Computing
Student Book

Alison Page
Diane Levine

OXFORD

Contents

Introduction 3

1 The nature of technology: Computers everyday 4
1.1 What is technology? 6
1.2 Staying safe 8
1.3 My computing family 10
1.4 Computers in school 12
1.5 Home and school 14
1.6 Being courteous 16
Check what you know 18

2 Digital literacy: Rainforests 20
2.1 Look at a web page 22
2.2 Find a web page 24
2.3 Find some facts 26
2.4 Using the browser 28
2.5 Are you feeling worried? 30
2.6 Staying safe 32
Check what you know 34

3 Computational thinking: Catch the mouse 36
3.1 Hello Scratch 38
3.2 Scratch on stage 40
3.3 Chase the mouse 42
3.4 What Scratch does 44
3.5 Think about input and output .. 46
3.6 The Hedgehog Game 48
Check what you know 50

4 Programming: Play with Scratch 52
4.1 Green flag means start 54
4.2 What is a sprite? 56
4.3 Costume change 58
4.4 Extra sprites 60
4.5 Find a new block 62
4.6 What Scratch says 64
Check what you know 66

5 Multimedia: Funny faces 68
5.1 The canvas 70
5.2 Drawing shapes 72
5.3 Erasing and undoing 74
5.4 Save for another time 76
5.5 Bring back your file 78
5.6 Move and swap 80
Check what you know 82

6 Numbers and data: Toys long ago 84
6.1 Toys from the past 86
6.2 Cells 88
6.3 Labels 90
6.4 Making a list 92
6.5 Number values 94
6.6 Editing 96
Check what you know 98
Glossary 100

Introduction

Delivering computing to young learners

Oxford International Primary and Lower Secondary Computing is a complete syllabus for computing education for ages 5–14 (Years 1–9). By following the program of learning set out in this series, teachers can feel reassured that their students have access to the computing skills and understanding that they need for their future education.

Find out more at:
www.oxfordprimary.com/computing.

Structure of the book

This book is divided into six chapters, for Year 1 (ages 5–6).

1. **The nature of technology:** Introduction to what computers are and how they help us
2. **Digital literacy:** Learning to use computers safely
3. **Computational thinking:** Thinking about how we control the computer
4. **Programming:** Running and editing a program
5. **Multimedia:** Making pictures with a computer
6. **Numbers and data:** Typing numbers with a computer

What you will find in each unit

- Introduction: An offline activity and a class discussion help students to start thinking about the topic.
- Lessons: Six lessons guide students through activity-based learning.
- Check what you know: A test and activities allow you to measure students' progress.

What you will find in the lessons

Although each lesson is unique, they have common features: learning outcomes for each lesson are set out at the start; learning content delivers skills and develops understanding.

Activity Every lesson involves a learning activity for the students.

Extra challenge Activities to extend students who are able to do more.

Think again Questions check students' understanding of the lesson.

Additional features

You will also find these features throughout the book:

Word cloud The word cloud builds vocabulary by identifying key terms from the unit.

Be creative Suggestions for creative and artistic work.

Explore more Extra tasks that can be taken outside the classroom and into the home.

Digital citizen of the future Advice on using computers responsibly in life.

Glossary Key terms are identified in the text and defined in the glossary at the end.

Assessing student achievement

The final pages in each unit give an opportunity to assess student achievement.

- Developing: This acknowledges the achievement of students who find the content challenging but have made progress.
- Secure: Students have reached the level set out in the programme for their age group. Most should reach this level.
- Extended: This recognises the achievement of students who have developed above-average skills and understanding.

Questions and activities are colour-coded according to achievement level. Self-evaluation advice helps students to check their own progress.

Software to use

We recommend Scratch for writing programs at this age. For other lessons, teachers can use any suitable software, for example: Microsoft Office; Google Drive software; LibreOffice; any web browser.

Source files

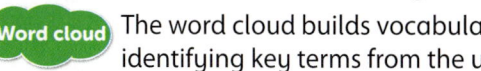 You will see this symbol on some of the pages.

This means that there are extra files you can access to help with the learning activities. For example, Scratch programming files and downloadable images.

To access the files, go to **www.oxfordowl.co.uk** and navigate to the 'Oxford International Primary Programme' page then 'Oxford International Primary Computing'.

Teacher's Guides

For more on these topics, look at the Teacher's Guide that accompanies this book.

1 The nature of technology: Computers everyday

You will learn
- what a computer is
- things we can do with computers
- how computers help us.

Computers are part of everyday life. In this unit you will learn what a computer is. You will learn how using computers can help you. You will learn how to stay safe when you are using a computer.

Talk about...
Have you ever seen a computer?
What did the computer look like?
Have you ever used a computer?
What did you use the computer for?

Learning outcomes: Say what a computer is; Say some things that can be done with a computer in school and out of school

Class activity

How can you stay safe and happy when you use computers at school?

Make a golden rule for using computers at school.

Make a poster of your rule.

> computer   mouse
> screen   keyboard
> laptop   courteous
> technology

Did you know?

Some people think the first computer was an abacus. The abacus was invented more than 2500 years ago in Babylon. An abacus is a counting machine.

1.1 What is technology?

In this lesson

You will learn:
→ how computers can help us.

Technology is any machine we can use to solve a problem.

A **computer** is a machine. Computers can do things quickly.

People tell computers what to do. We can use computers to help us...

Play

Work

Talk

Parts of a computer

A computer has different parts.

Screen
Mouse
Keyboard

This computer looks different. It is a **laptop**.

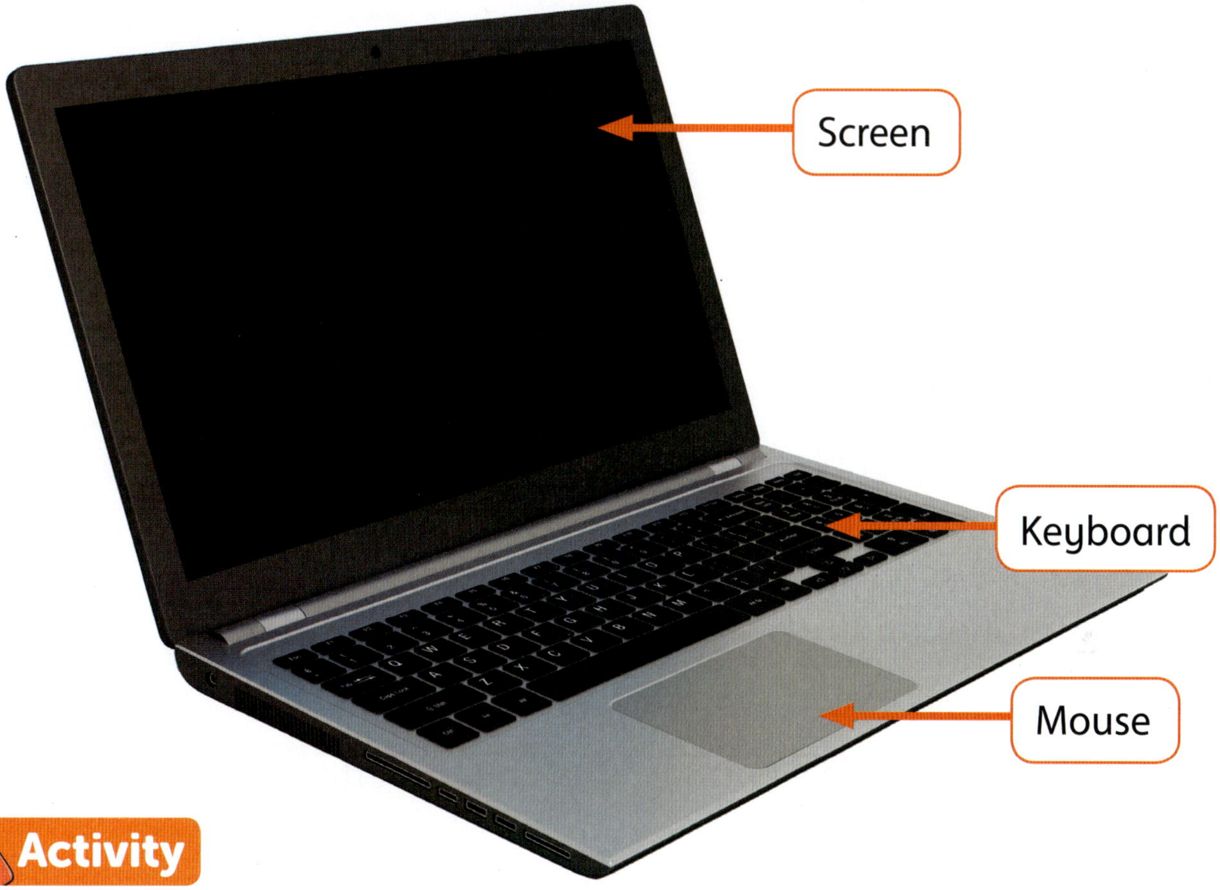

Screen

Keyboard

Mouse

Activity

Draw a picture of a computer. In your picture, show:

- the screen
- the mouse
- the keyboard.

Extra challenge

What is this?

Explore more

Talk to someone at home about technologies they use. Draw pictures. Bring your pictures to school.

1.2 Staying safe

In this lesson

You will learn:
→ how to stay safe when you are using a computer.

The girl is using a computer.

There is no food or drink near the computer. The girl is sitting on a chair. She can see the **screen**. She can use the **mouse**. She can reach the **keyboard**.

A keyboard has buttons on it.

What can you see on the buttons? Can you see letters, numbers and symbols?

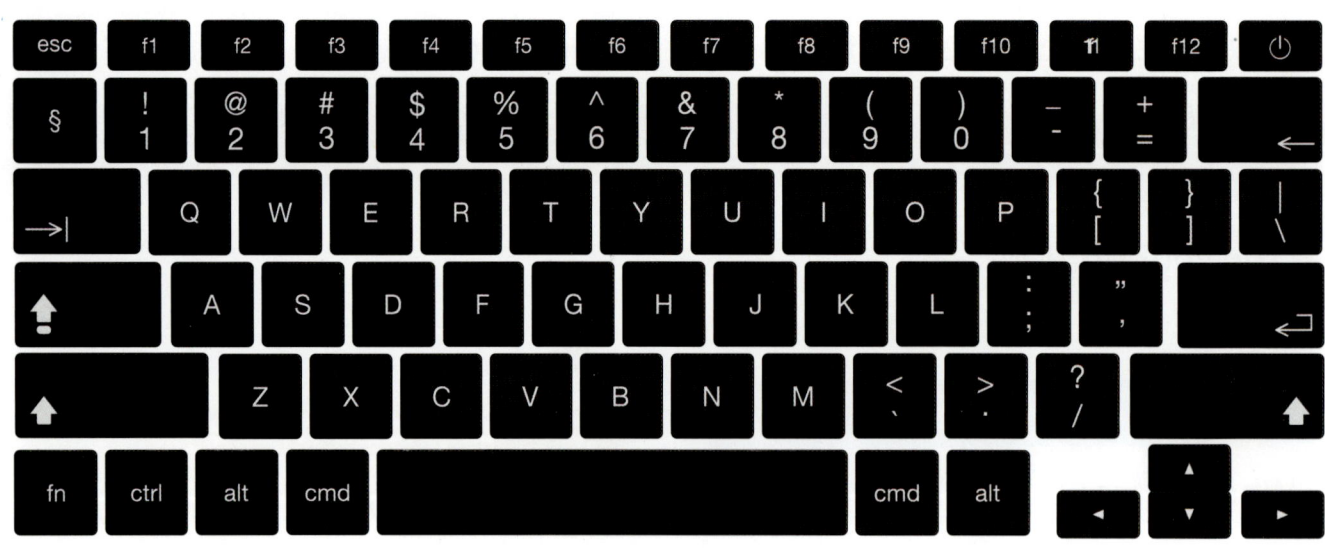

Think again Is your keyboard like the one in the picture? What is the same? What is different?

Activity

What is wrong with the way these children are using their computers?

Extra challenge

These children are sharing nicely. What could they do to be safer?

1 The nature of technology: Computers everyday

1.3 My computing family

In this lesson

You will learn:

→ how people use computers at home.

You have asked someone outside school how they use computers. What did they say?

"I use computers to find things out."

"I use computers to play games."

"I use computers to work."

"We use computers to talk to people in our family."

 **Activity**

Draw a picture of one thing you can do with a computer outside school. For example, make a picture of a car.

Give your picture to your teacher.

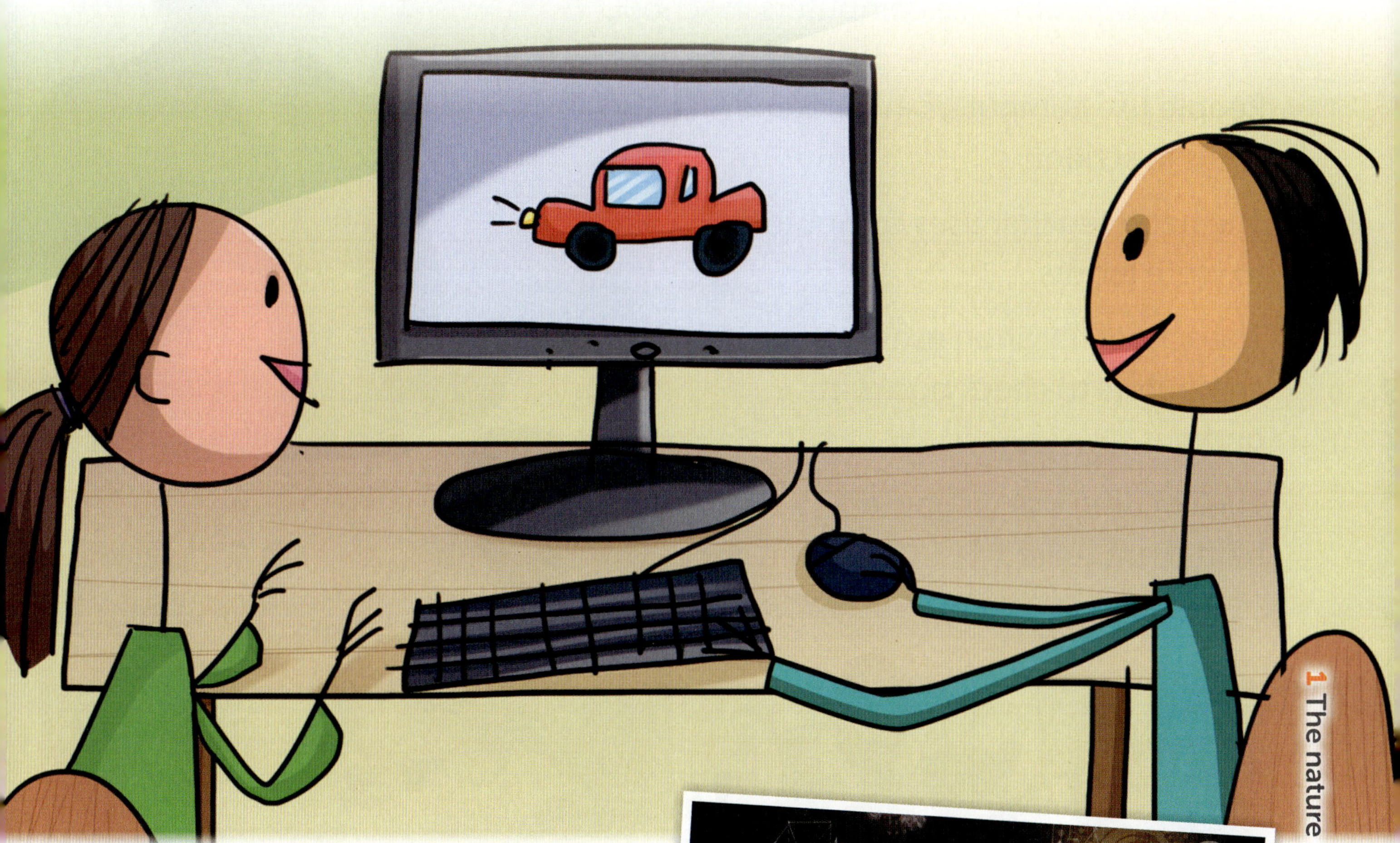

 **Extra challenge**

What else could you do with a computer outside school?

 How will you use computers when you are grown up?

1.4 Computers in school

In this lesson

You will learn:

→ how people use computers in school.

People use computers in different ways in school.

The head teacher uses computers to write letters.

The school librarian uses computers to check books in and out.

The children use computers to help them learn.

The office worker uses a computer to help run the school.

 **Activity**

Walk around the school with some classmates.

Ask the people you meet how they use computers.

Draw pictures of the ways people use computers in school.

Think again How do you think computers make it easier for adults to do their jobs in school?

 Extra challenge

Write one sentence about the ways adults use computers in school.

Digital citizen of the future

Do you think you will use a computer in your job when you are an adult?

1.5 Home and school

In this lesson

You will learn:

→ how to compare the ways people use computers inside and outside school.

In a group, draw a big circle on a large piece of paper, like this:

Now draw another big circle like this:

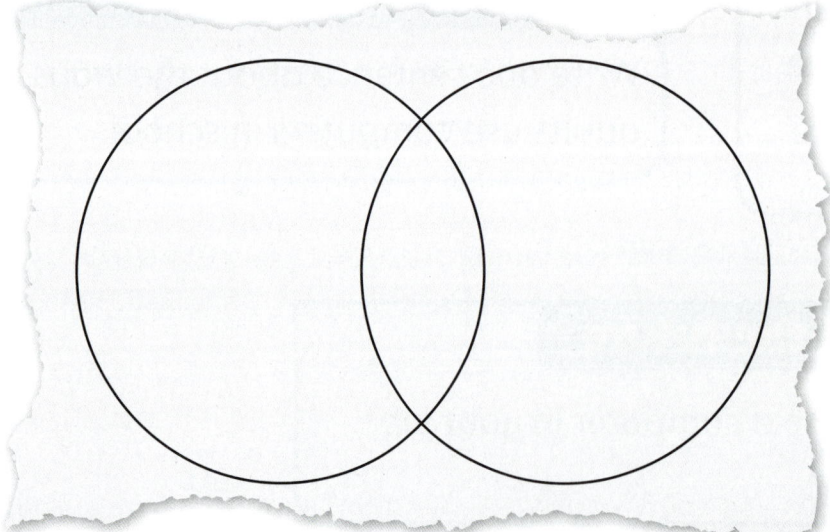

Look at the pictures you have drawn of people using computers.

Put all the pictures of people using computers outside school in one circle.

Put all the pictures of people using computers inside school in the other circle.

How do people use computers inside school?

How do people use computers outside school?

 **Extra challenge**

Which pictures fit inside the middle of the circles?

 What do you like to do on a computer?

1.6 Being courteous

In this lesson

You will learn:
→ how to be courteous when you use computers.

Sometimes people use computers to do the wrong thing.

We need to be **courteous** when we use computers. Being courteous means being polite and thinking about other people.

 **Activity**

In a group, talk about these problems. What would you do if:

- someone sends you a text message that makes you unhappy?
- someone you know answers their phone while you are talking to them?
- two people are arguing over one computer?
- someone sends you a message with an angry emoji?

Digital citizen of the future

When we use computers we should only write things we would say to the person if they were standing in front of us.

 Extra challenge

Have you ever had a problem when you used computers? What was your problem? How did you solve it?

Check what you know

You have learned
- what a computer is
- things we can do with computers
- how computers help us.

Test

Show or tell to answer these questions.

1 Can you use a computer safely? Show or tell your teacher.

2 Say one way a grown-up might use a computer outside of school.

3 Say how computers can help people.

 **Activities**

1. Draw a picture of:
   - a computer screen
   - a keyboard
   - a computer mouse.
2. Write the names of the computer parts onto your picture.

Self-evaluation

- I answered test question 1.
- I can use a computer at school.
- I answered test questions 1 and 2.
- I did activity 1.
- I answered all the test questions.
- I did activities 1 and 2.

Re-read any parts of the unit you feel unsure about. Try the test and activities again – can you do more this time?

2 Digital literacy: Rainforests

You will learn
- how to find something out using the computer
- to be safe and polite in the computer room
- who can help you if you are worried.

In this unit you will use the internet to find out about the Amazon rainforest. You will learn how to stay safe and happy when you use computers and the internet.

You will also make a poster to share information about the rainforest.

Talk about…
What kind of place do you live in?

Is it a forest? Is it a desert? Is it a town?

Learning outcomes: Find something out using the computer; Be safe and polite in the computer room; Say who can help you if you are worried

Class activity

The Amazon rainforest is in South America. The rainforest is big! The long river that flows through the forest is called the Amazon River.

The rainforest is important to our whole planet. Many plants and animals live in the rainforest.

Some people do not look after the rainforest.

Look at pictures of a rainforest. What do you see that interests you?

internet   web page
website   hyperlink
browser   content
menu   search engine
scrolling

Did you know?

Nine different countries are home to the Amazon rainforest.

2.1 Look at a web page

In this lesson

You will learn:

→ what a web page is.

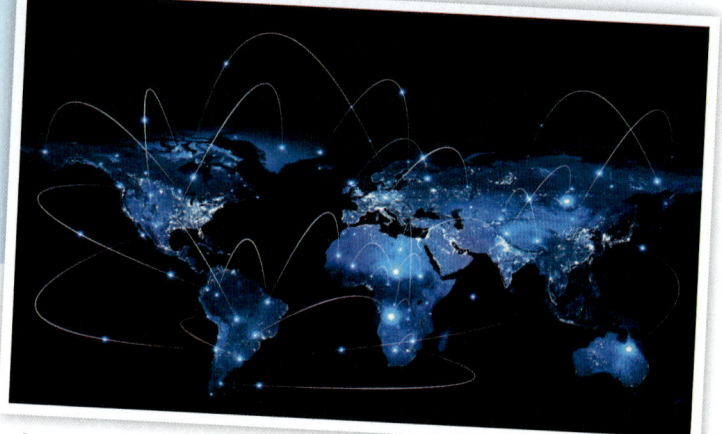

What is a web page?

Computers all over the world are connected. We call these connected computers the **internet.**

People make **web pages**. Using the internet you can look at web pages people made.

Your teacher will help you open a web page. Here is an example. Yours might be different.

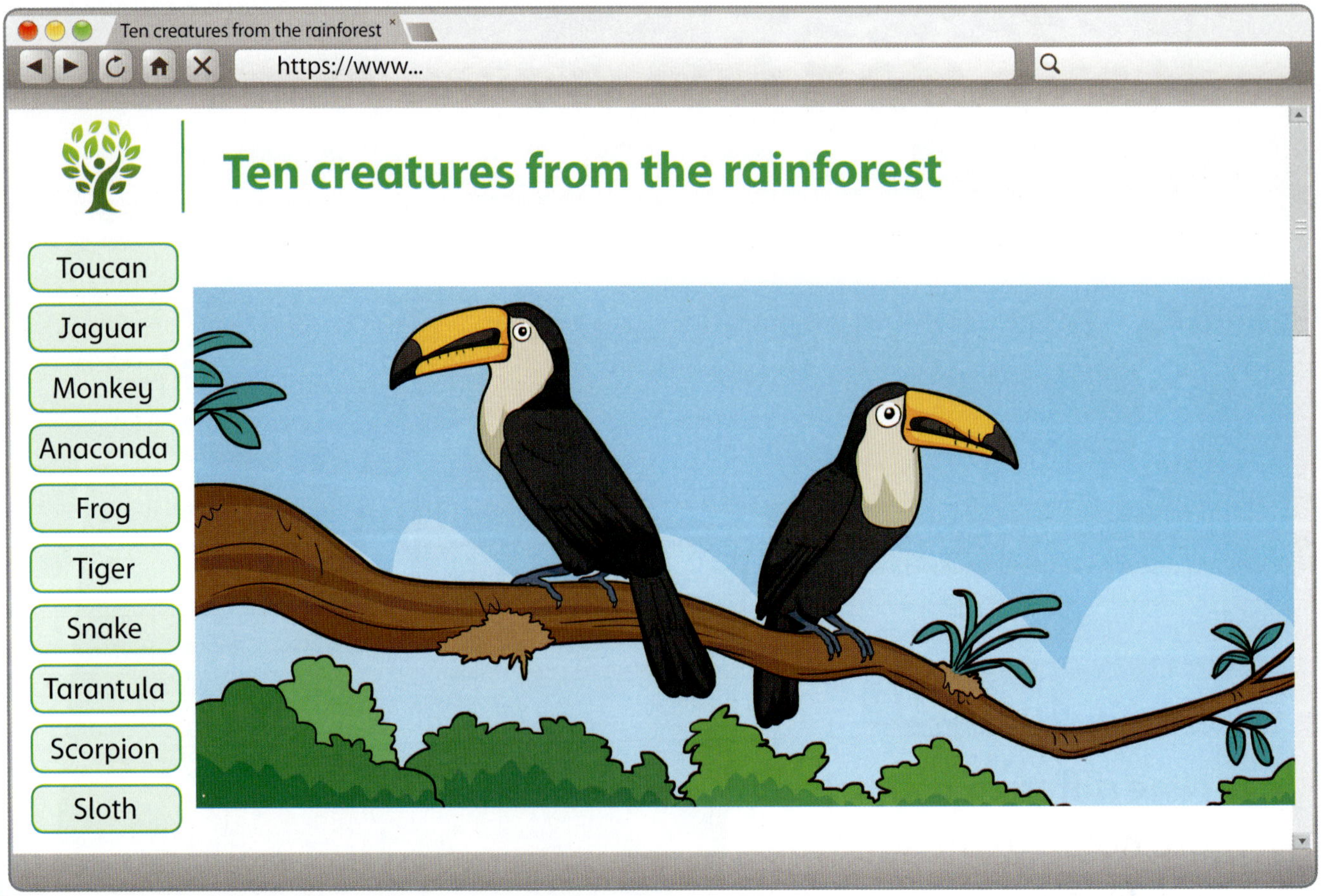

Ten creatures from the rainforest
https://www...
Ten creatures from the rainforest
Toucan
Jaguar
Monkey
Anaconda
Frog
Tiger
Snake
Tarantula
Scorpion
Sloth

Scrolling

This web page has many pictures. You can't see them all at once. **Scrolling** is a way to look through a big page. Turn the wheel on your mouse.

This is the mouse wheel.

Look at a web page about rainforest animals.

Draw a picture of something you can see on this web page.

Extra challenge

Read any words on the web page.

Write about what you found out from this web page.

Think again

If you could make a web page on any topic, what would you choose? Write or draw to show your answer.

2.2 Find a web page

In this lesson

You will learn:

→ how to find a web page.

You can find more web pages to look at. A special web page called a **search engine** will help you find pages you like.

Your teacher will help you open this web page: www.kiddle.co

There is a white box at the bottom of the screen. Type the name of your favourite animal in this box.

This student typed: 'tiger'.

You will see **links** to web pages. The links are the blue words. If you click on a link a new web page will open.

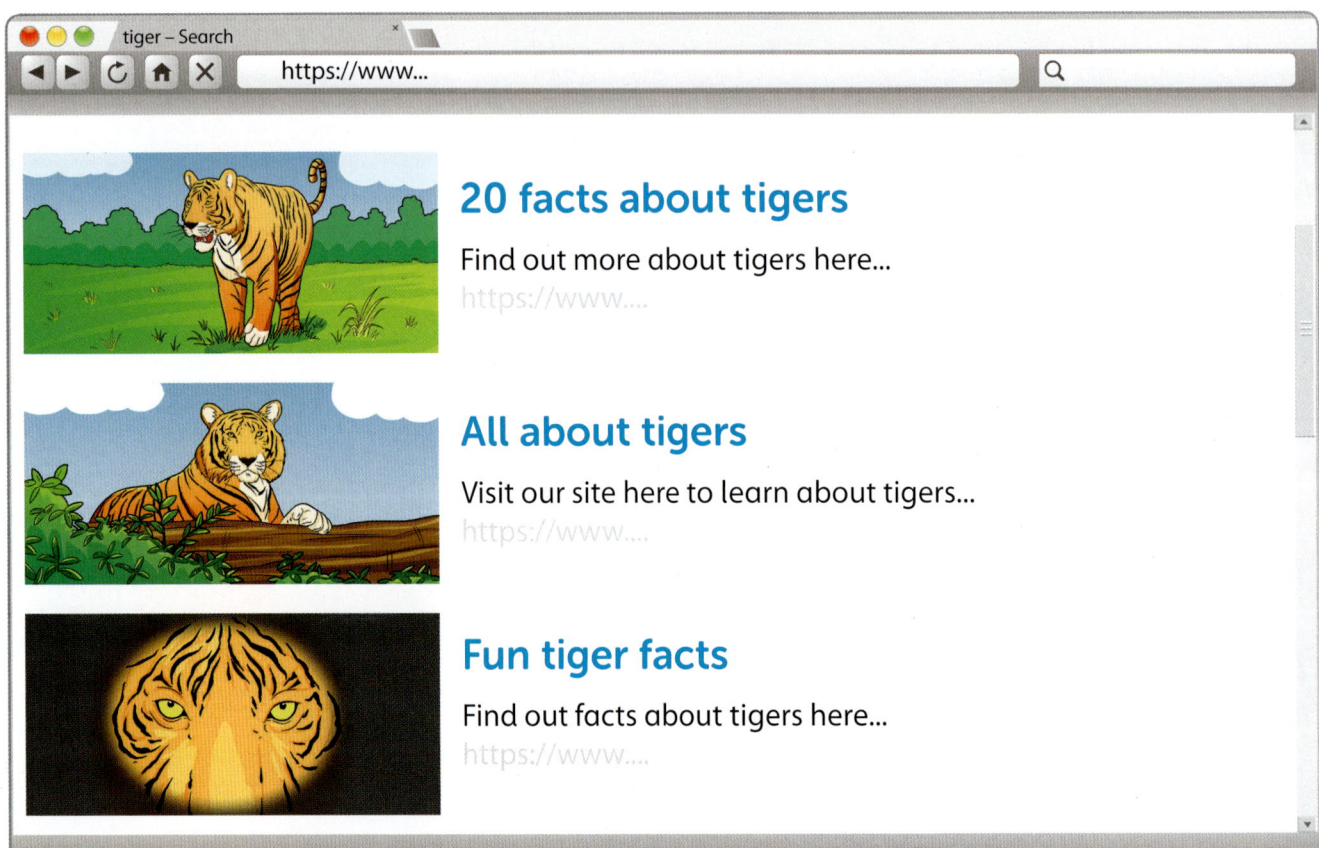

The student clicked on 'Fun tiger facts' and saw this page.

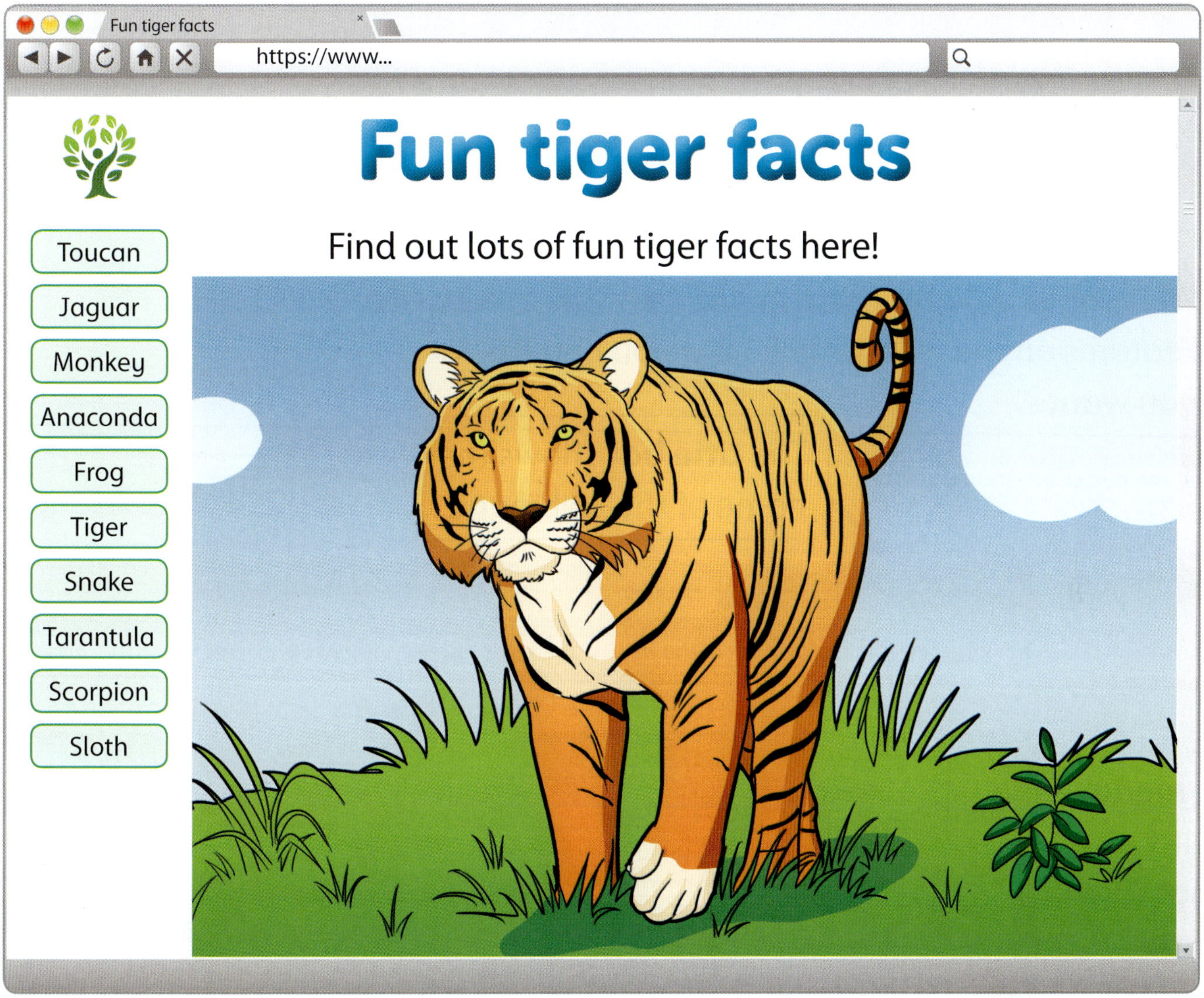

Fun tiger facts

Find out lots of fun tiger facts here!

- Toucan
- Jaguar
- Monkey
- Anaconda
- Frog
- Tiger
- Snake
- Tarantula
- Scorpion
- Sloth

Activity

Find a web page about an animal you like. Draw a picture of what you found.

Extra challenge

Read about the animal you like. Make a word list about that animal.

Explore more

Click on different links to look at more web pages. Draw or write about what you found.

2.3 Find some facts

In this lesson

You will learn:
→ how to find useful facts on a website.

Web pages are grouped together to make a **website**. Features on the website will help you find the facts you want.

The **title bar** shows the name of the web page.

The **menu** is a list of things that you can choose on a website.

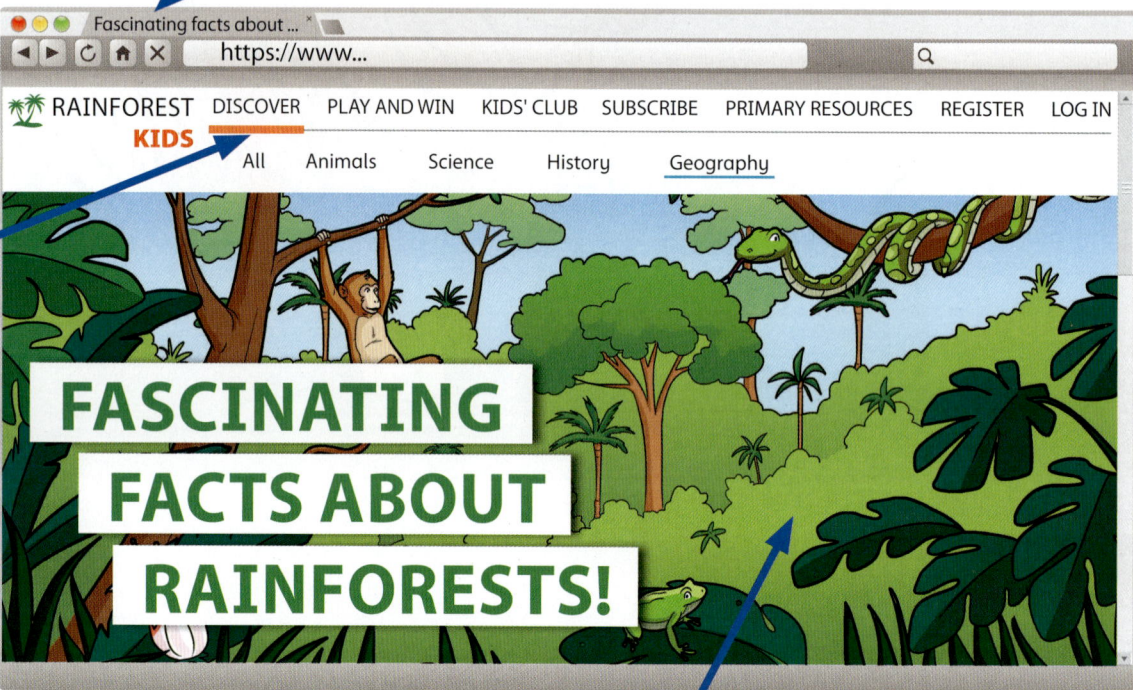

This is the **content**. Content is anything we see or create on the internet.

What is the menu?

Have you been to a restaurant? You can choose food and drink from a list called a menu.

The menu on a web page will help you choose other pages on the same website.

Click here to go to find out more about the topics.

Click here to play games.

Some links may be harder to read. Ask an adult for help.

This is called a **drop-down menu**. Click to learn about monkeys, snakes or frogs.

Activity

Use a search engine.

In the search box type: rainforest.

Find one fact about rainforests.

Extra challenge

Use website features to find out more facts.

Be creative

Draw a picture of a web page. Remember, you will need a title bar, a menu and some content.

Write about the facts you found in this lesson.

2.4 Using the browser

In this lesson

You will learn:
→ how to move around the web.

The software you have used to look at web pages is called a **browser**. Features of the browser will help you look at a website.

A website can have more than one page.

One way to move to a new web page is to click on a **hyperlink**.

A hyperlink is an electronic link. The link allows you to move from one place on a website to another place on the same website, or a different website.

A hyperlink can be made of letters. They might be underlined or **bold** or a **different colour**. A picture can be a hyperlink, too.

How to use links

Look at this website.

The pictures of animals are links. Click on the toucan.

Now you see this on the screen.

Here it is!

If you want, you can go back again. Use the arrow buttons on your browser. You can go forward and back.

Activity

Find out about an animal in the rainforest.

Use a hyperlink.

Use the forward and back icons.

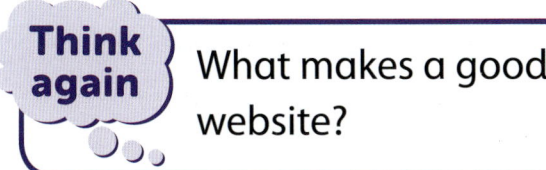

What makes a good website?

Extra challenge

Find out one way we can help look after rainforests.

2.5 Are you feeling worried?

In this lesson

You will learn:

→ what to do if you feel worried about something you see online.

These children are doing a project on rainforest animals.

The children have clicked on a hyperlink. They have seen some pictures of animals losing their homes.

The children are worried. They can:

Tell a teacher or an adult they trust.

You can use the report button or click on the word 'Report' on a page.

The report button tells the right people that there is something scary or worrying on a web page.

 **Activity**

Make a poster to tell other children what to do if they are worried about something they see on a web page.

 **Extra challenge**

Make a poster about a rainforest animal.

 **Think again**

Make a list of people you could tell if something worries you on a web page.

🔘 **Digital citizen of the future**

What could you do if your classmate tells you they have seen something online that has scared or worried them?

2.6 Staying safe

In this lesson

You will learn:
→ how to stay safe when you use the internet.

The internet is like a market or shop, with lots of people.

Information about your life is called **personal information**. For example, your name, your address or your school is personal information.

You would not tell personal information to a stranger in a shop. On the internet you must not share personal information with people you do not know.

Personal information can be words.

Personal information can be pictures.

If someone asks you for personal information, tell an adult you trust right away.

 **Activity**

Make a drawing or write about being safe on the internet.

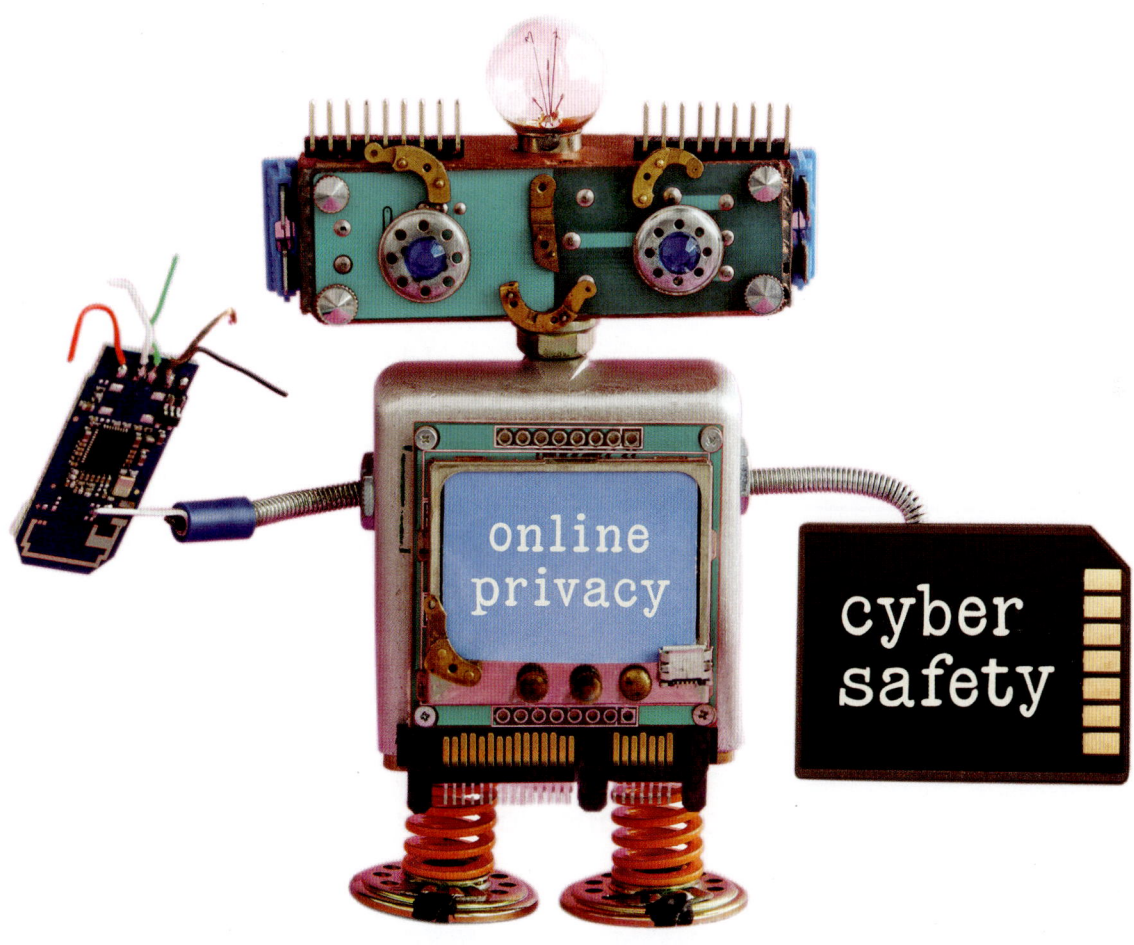

 Extra challenge

Use your fact-finding skills. Find out how many people use the internet.

 Say or write what you would do if someone on the internet asked for personal information.

Check what you know

You have learned
→ how to find things out using the computer
→ to be safe and polite in the computer room
→ who can help you if you are worried.

Test

A student saw something that worried them on a web page.

1. Show or tell what you would do.
2. Write the name of a grown-up you would tell if you were worried.
3. Say one thing that is personal information.

Activities

1. Look at pictures of butterflies on a web page.
2. Draw a picture to show one thing you saw on a web page.
3. Write an interesting fact about butterflies.

Self-evaluation

- I answered test question 1.
- I did activity 1.
- I answered test questions 1 and 2.
- I did activities 1 and 2.
- I answered all the test questions.
- I did all the activities.

Re-read any parts of the unit you feel unsure about. Try the test and activities again – can you do more this time?

3 Computational thinking: Catch the mouse

You will learn

→ to use the mouse to control the computer

→ to use the keyboard to control the computer

→ what inputs are

→ to see and hear outputs.

In this unit you will use a computer. You will use the computer mouse. You will make a cat move on the screen.

 **Class activity**

A computer **mouse** looks like this. You can move it on the table.

Have you used a computer mouse before?

Draw a picture to show how you used the mouse.

Learning outcomes: Run and use a simple program made by someone else; Describe a program by saying what its inputs and outputs are

input   output
Scratch   game
mouse pointer

Talk about…

Some computers don't have a mouse. You touch the screen instead. Have you ever done that?

Did you know?

Doug Engelbart invented the computer mouse. His friends asked why he called it a mouse. He said, "Because it looks like a little mouse with a tail." Does your mouse have a tail or not?

3.1 Hello Scratch

In this lesson

You will learn:

→ about **Scratch**. Scratch is a programming language for children.

This is Scratch the cat. He will help you learn.

Scratch will walk when you click with the mouse. Scratch walks inside a square. The square is called the **stage**.

You will work with the Scratch website.

https://scratch.mit.edu/projects/editor/

A program is ready to use. The program tells Scratch to walk.

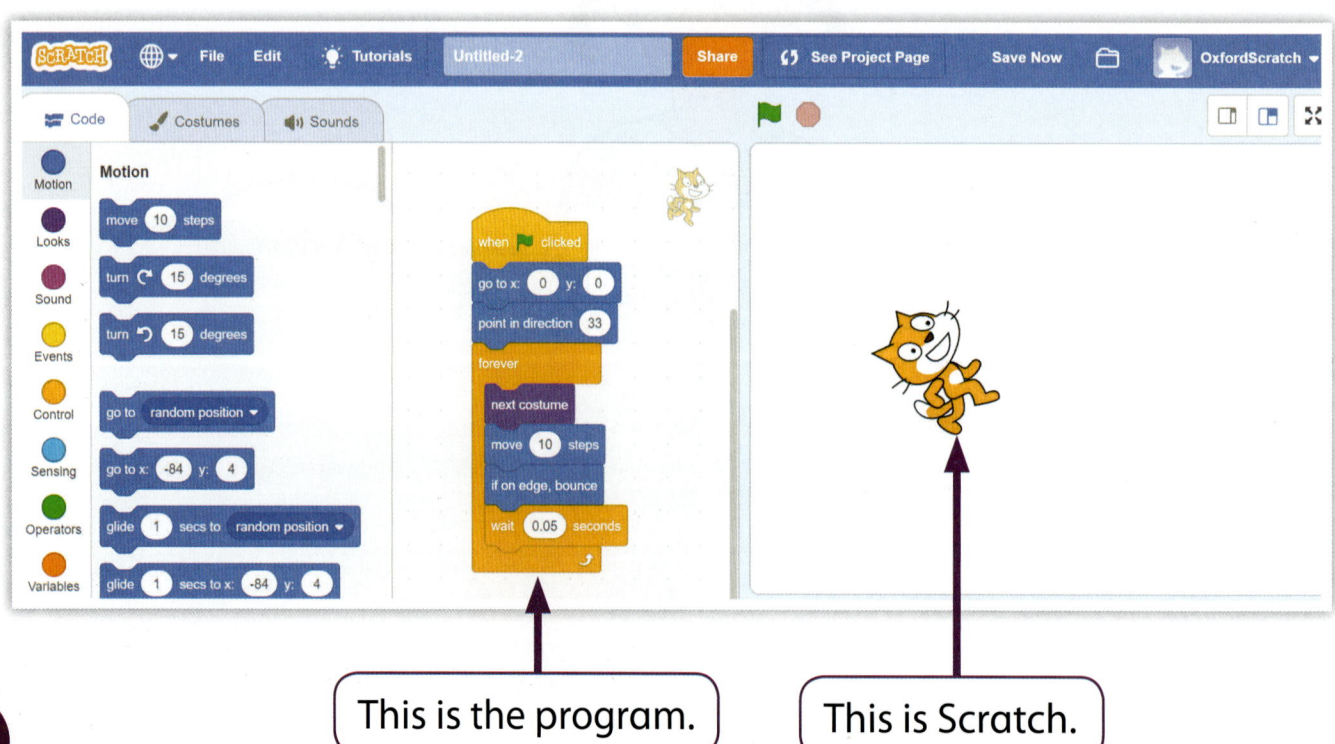

This is the program.   This is Scratch.

Icons are little pictures. They show you things the computer can do.

To use an icon do this:

1 Move the mouse pointer to the icon.

2 Click the icon.

There are two icons at the top of the stage. They look like this.

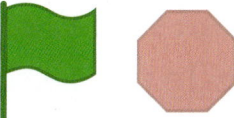

The green flag makes the program start. The red button makes the program stop.

1 Move the mouse pointer to the green flag. Click on the green flag to make Scratch walk.

2 Move the mouse pointer to the red button. Click on the red button to make Scratch stop.

> **Think again** Look at the program. The program is made of blocks.
>
> What is the picture on the first block? Why do you think the block shows that picture?
>
>

3.2 Scratch on stage

In this lesson

You will learn:

→ how to make changes to the Scratch stage.

Last lesson you used the 'start' and 'stop' icons. By clicking the icons you could start and stop the program. Scratch walked on the stage. In this lesson you will make changes to the stage.

You can change the size of the stage.

This icon makes the stage big. Move the pointer to the icon. Click the mouse button.

This icon makes the stage small.

Click on this icon. Make the stage small again.

You can change the **backdrop**.

The stage can have a picture on it. The picture is called the backdrop.

This icon lets you change the backdrop.

Click here to choose a new backdrop.

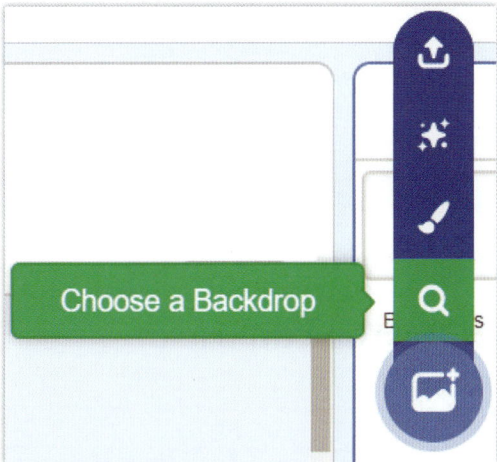

Click on any picture.

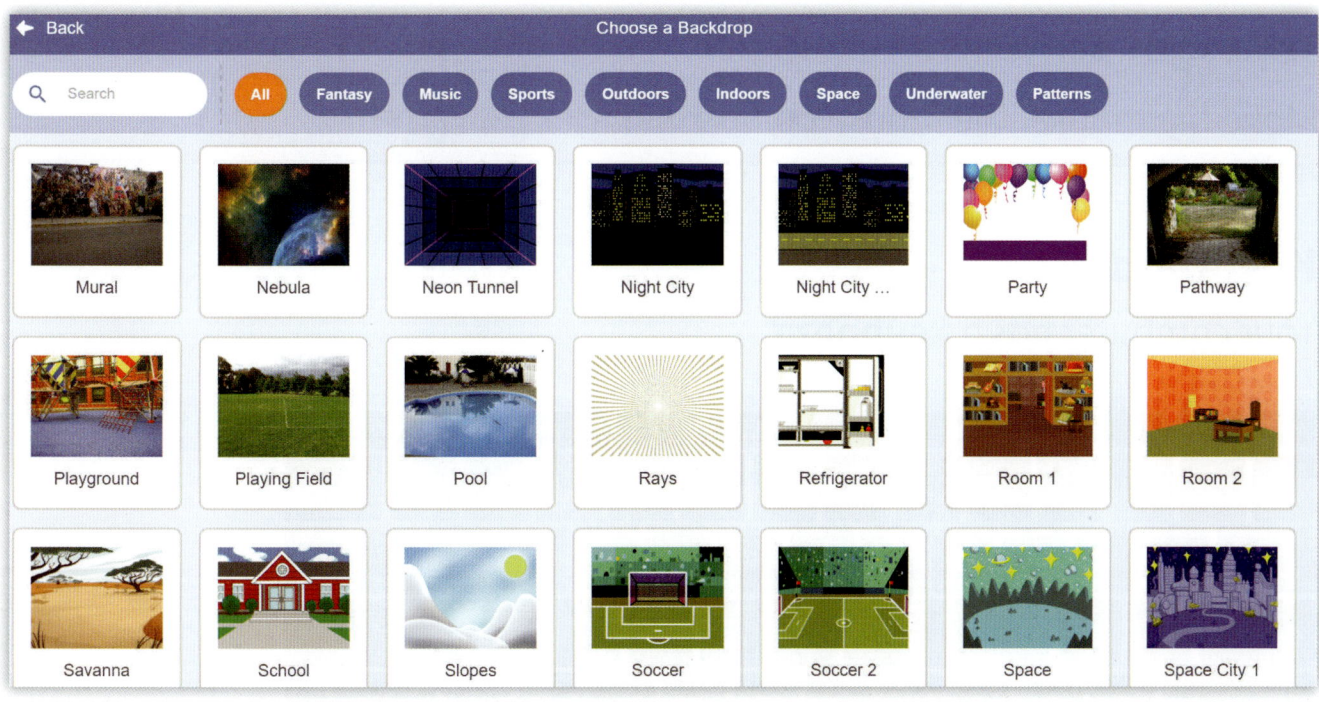

What does the stage look like now?

Be creative

Think of a new backdrop for Scratch. Paint a picture to show your idea.

3.3 Chase the mouse

In this lesson

You will learn:

→ about input.

Input is how you control the computer. You can use a:

- mouse
- keyboard.

Mouse

The **mouse pointer** is on the screen.

Move the mouse. The mouse pointer will move too.

Keyboard

Your computer has a **keyboard**.

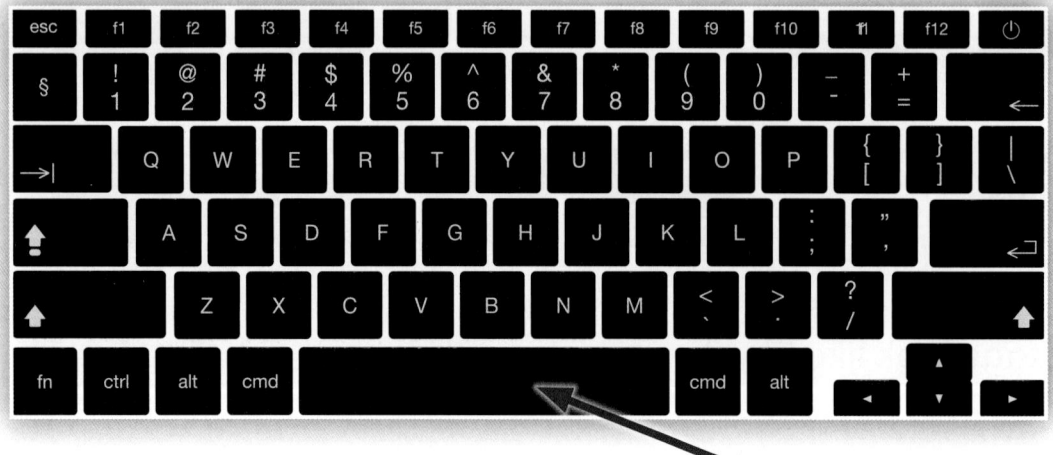

Space bar

The keyboard lets you type letters.

Activity

You can move the mouse. Press the space bar. Scratch will start to walk.

Move the mouse pointer. Scratch will chase after it.

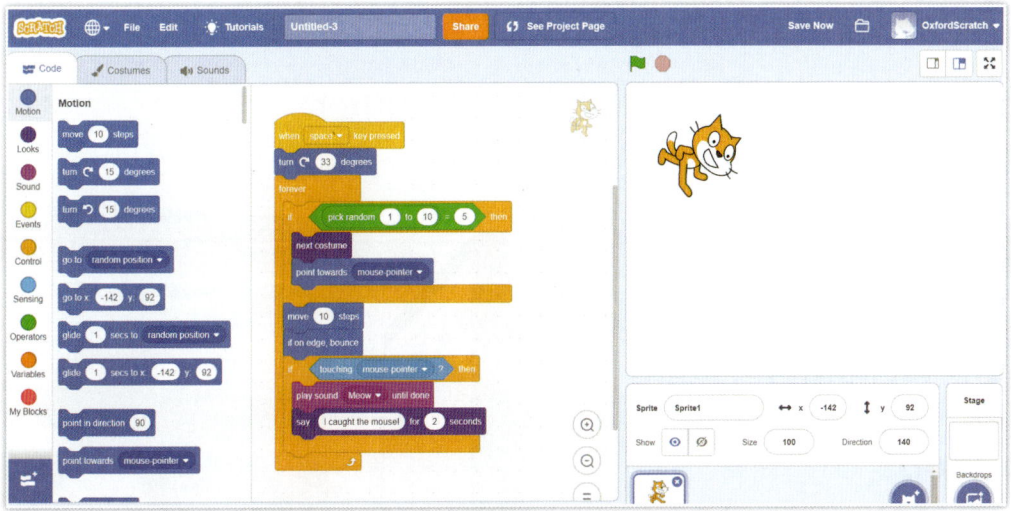

Keep moving the mouse pointer.
Don't let Scratch catch it.

Think again

You have learned two ways to control the computer.

Draw or write to show these two ways.

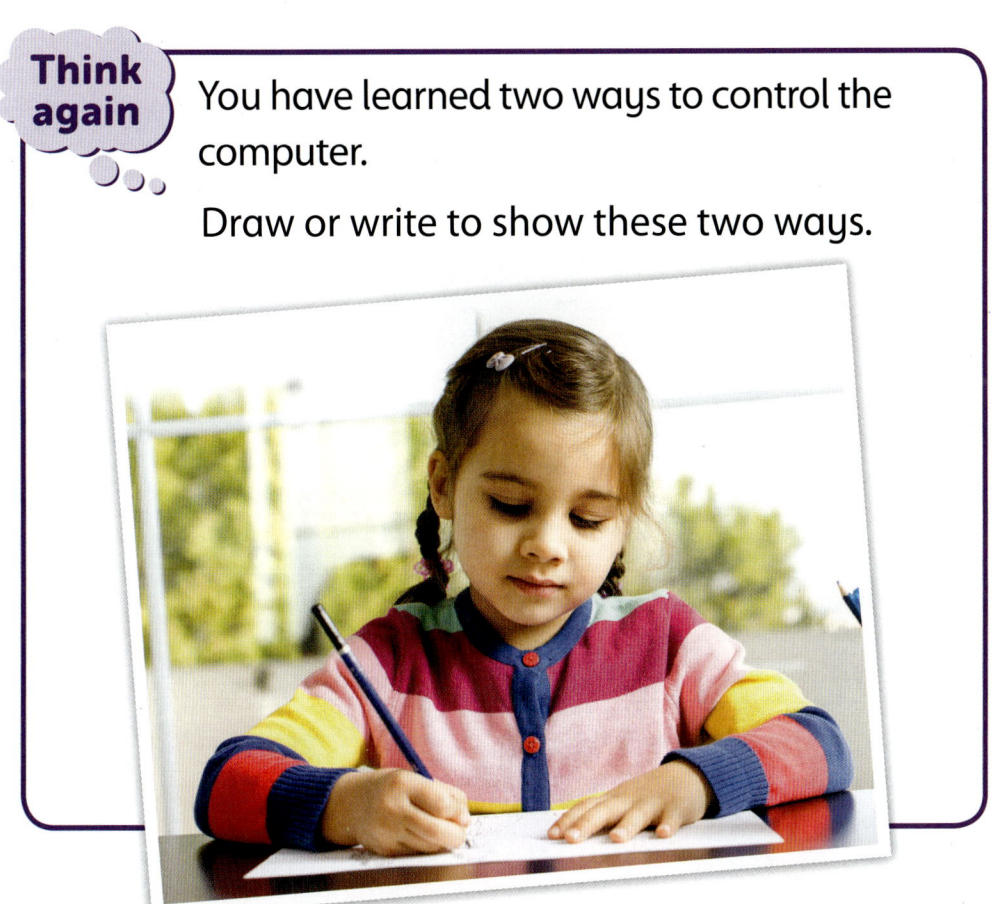

3.4 What Scratch does

In this lesson

You will learn:

→ about output.

Output comes out of the computer. The computer makes output. You can see or hear output.

Visual output

You can see some output. You see output on the computer screen.

Sound output

You can hear some output. You can listen on headphones. Or the sound might come out of the computer.

 **Activity**

Press the space bar. The program starts. Scratch will chase the mouse pointer.

Let Scratch catch the mouse pointer.

What do you see on the screen?

What do you hear?

I caught the mouse!

Think again Draw and write to show the two outputs from this program.

Digital citizen of the future

Is it noisy in your classroom when lots of children use this program? Scratch has a loud meow. Sound output can be noisy. Listening on headphones means you don't disturb anyone else.

3.5 Think about input and output

In this lesson

You will learn:

→ to think about input and output.

Input is what you do to control the computer.

Output is what comes out of the computer. The computer makes the output.

The Scratch program you used had input and output.

 **Activity**

To make input you used:

- keyboard
- mouse.

Draw a picture to show the two types of input.

 **Activity**

There are two outputs:
- visual output
- sound output.

Draw a picture to show the two types of output.

 **Extra challenge**

Add word labels to your pictures. How can you control the program?

 **Explore more**

Different types of computer have different inputs and outputs. Find out as many different kinds as you can.

Be creative

Some people have never used a computer. Think of a person like that. Write a letter to them. Tell them how you use a computer at school. Draw a picture to show them.

3.6 The Hedgehog Game

In this lesson

You will learn:

→ to control the computer using inputs.

In this lesson you will play a **game**. It is called the Hedgehog Game. This game has two animals in it. They are Scratch the cat and a hedgehog.

- Scratch will follow the mouse pointer.
- The hedgehog will walk up and down.

A hedgehog is a spiky animal. If Scratch touches the hedgehog he will say "Ouch!".

Help Scratch to keep away from the hedgehog.

 Activity

- Press any key to start the game.
- Press the space bar to make the hedgehog walk.
- Move the mouse so Scratch walks carefully.

Ouch!

 **Be creative**

Choose a backdrop for the Hedgehog Game.

 **Think again** What are the inputs and outputs of this game? Draw or write to show them.

 Extra challenge

Talk about other computer games you know. What were the inputs and outputs? Draw or write to show them.

Check what you know

You have learned
- to use the mouse to control the computer
- to use the keyboard to control the computer
- what inputs are
- to see and hear outputs.

Test

Here are some parts of a computer.

Mouse

Headphones

Screen

Keyboard

1. Point to a part that is used for input.
2. Draw or write any part that is used for output.
3. Draw a picture of a computer. Include all the parts used for input and output.

Activities

1. Play the Hedgehog Game (or any other game on a computer).

   Let your teacher see you work carefully at the computer.

2. Tell the teacher what you did.

3. Tell the teacher how you controlled the computer.

Self-evaluation

- I answered test question 1.
- I did activity 1 quietly and safely.
- I answered test questions 1 and 2.
- I did activities 1 and 2.
- I answered all the test questions.
- I did all the activities.

Re-read any parts of the unit you feel unsure about. Try the test and activities again – can you do more this time?

Digital citizen of the future

Computer games are good fun. But don't play a game when you are supposed to be working in class.

4 Programming: Play with Scratch

You will learn
→ about blocks that make a program
→ to make changes to a program.

In this unit you will look at a program made of blocks. You will learn how programs are made. You will make changes to the program.

Scratch the cat is a **sprite**.

In the last unit you added a hedgehog sprite.

There are many other sprites. Here are some.

Which type of sprite do you like best?

Learning outcomes: Edit a program and say how that will change what it does

 **Digital citizen of the future**

We often use programs that other people made. But we can also make changes. We can make programs do just what we want.

sprite   block
program   drag
right-click

Be creative

Think of a new sprite that could be friends with Scratch. Draw the new sprite.

Did you know?

There are tutorials on the Scratch website. Look at the tutorials if you want to learn extra skills.

Getting Started

Create Animations That Talk

Animate an Adventure Game

Animate a Name

Make Music

Make a Clicker Game

Talk about…

What computer games do you know? Which are your favourites?

4.1 Green flag means start

In this lesson

You will learn:

→ to make a program start.

A **program** means some instructions. The instructions tell the computer what to do.

Look at this screen. In the middle of the screen is a program. The program is made of **blocks**. The blocks are shapes that fit together. Each block makes the computer do one thing.

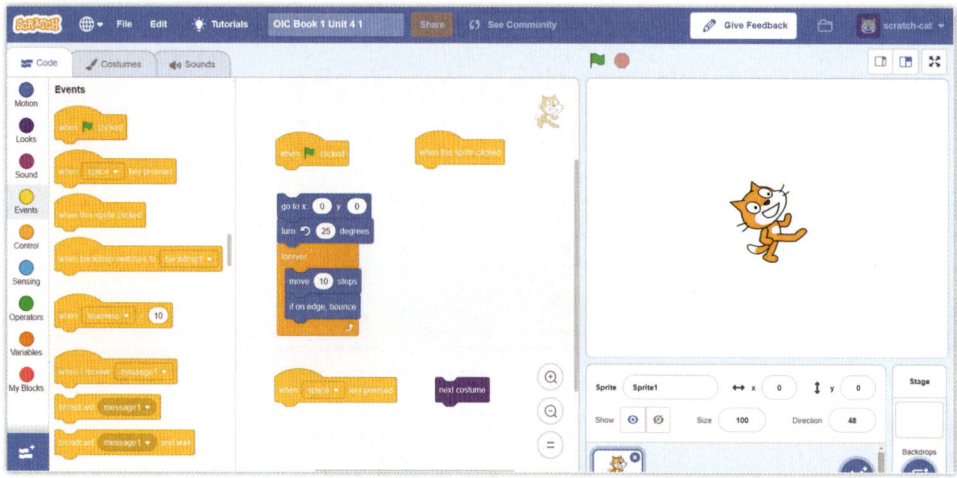

This block tells the computer to start the program. It has a green flag on it.

You can move the blocks and fit them together.

To move a block do this:

1. Move the mouse pointer to the block.
2. Press your finger on the mouse button. Keep pressing.
3. Move the mouse.

The block will move along too. This is called **dragging** the block.

When the block is in the right place, let go of the mouse pointer. The block will drop into the new place. This is called **drag and drop**.

Drag the green flag block to the program. When it touches the program the blocks will join together. It is like a jigsaw puzzle. Here is what the program will look like.

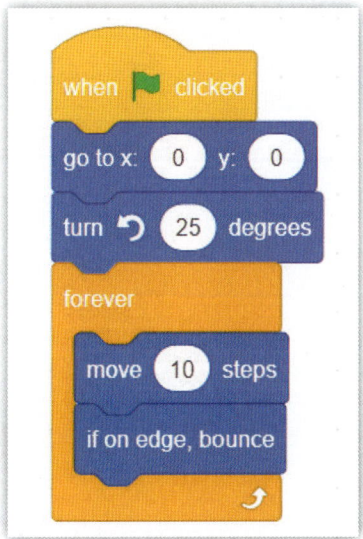

You joined the green flag block to the program.

Now click the green flag. The program will start. Scratch the cat will walk about.

 Extra challenge

You learned how to add a backdrop to a program. Give this program a backdrop.

 Explain what you did in this lesson. What change did you make? What happened?

4.2 What is a sprite?

In this lesson

You will learn:
- how to make a program start in a new way
- what a sprite is.

A **sprite** is a picture on screen. A program makes the sprite move. Scratch is a sprite.

The program looks like this.

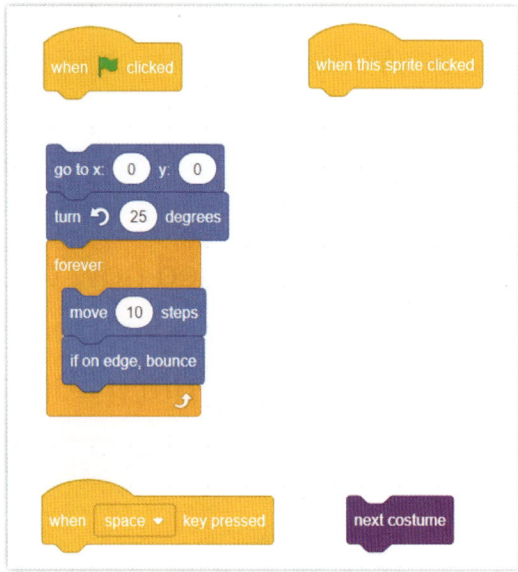

Some blocks have a curved top. A block with a curved top is a **start block**. A start block makes the program start.

Here are two start blocks.

One has got the green flag. The other one says 'when this sprite clicked'.

 **Activity**

Join the second block to the program.

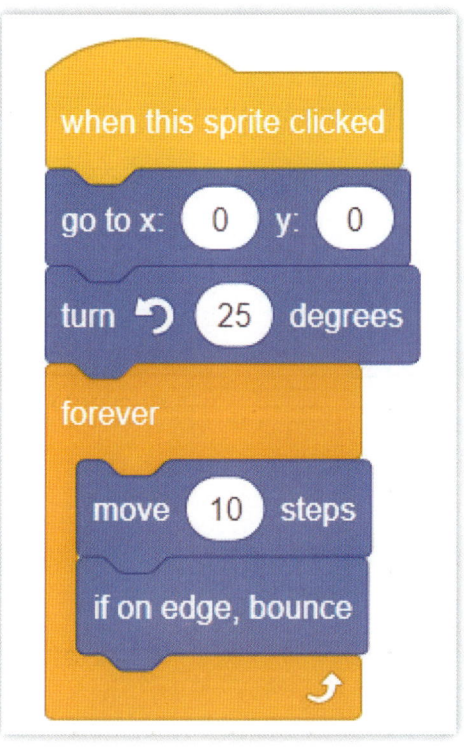

 **Extra challenge**

There is another start block on the screen. Can you find it? What happens if you use this start block?

 **Think again** What is a sprite? Say in your own words.

Click on the green flag. Nothing happens.

Click on the sprite. The program will start.

The sprite will move on the empty screen. Or on a backdrop if you chose one. This picture is an example.

4 Programming: Play with Scratch

57

4.3 Costume change

In this lesson

You will learn:

→ to add a new block to the program.

Fit the program to a start block. You can choose which one.

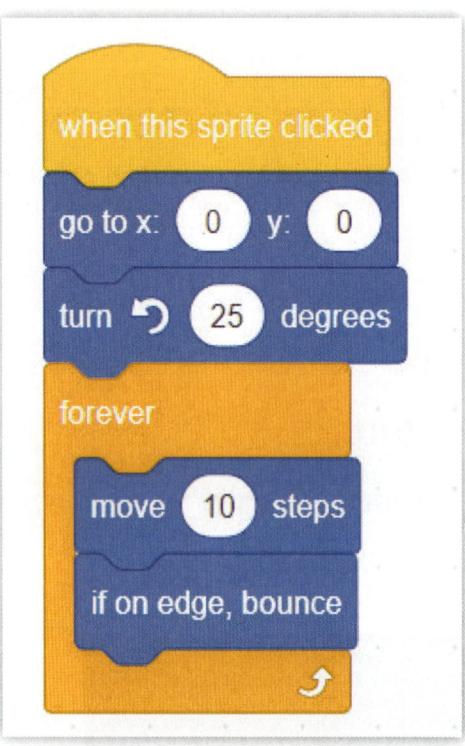

There is a purple block on the screen. Now you will add that block to the program.

Purple blocks change how Scratch looks. Scratch can swap between two looks. The looks are called **costumes**.

Changing costumes makes Scratch's legs move about. This block says 'next costume'.

You will fit the purple costume block into the program. First you must pull the blocks apart.

Then you can add the purple costume block. Make sure you put the it in the right place.

Then you can put the blocks back together again.

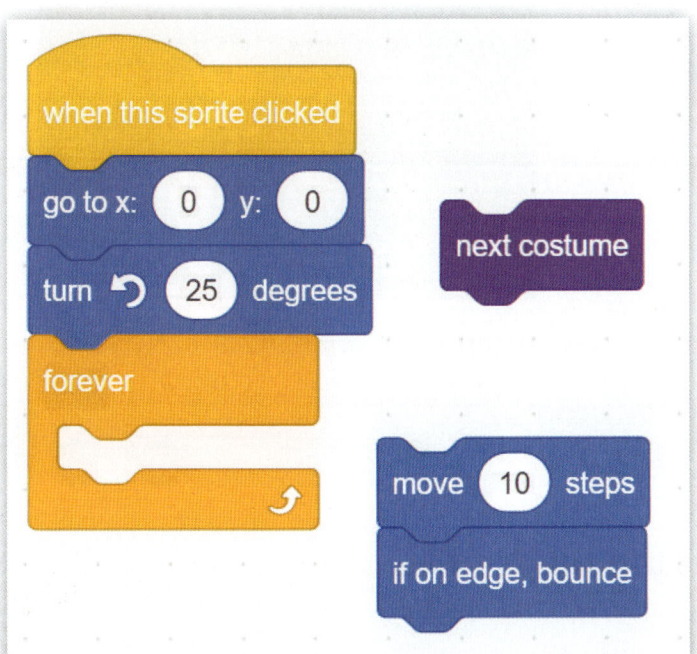 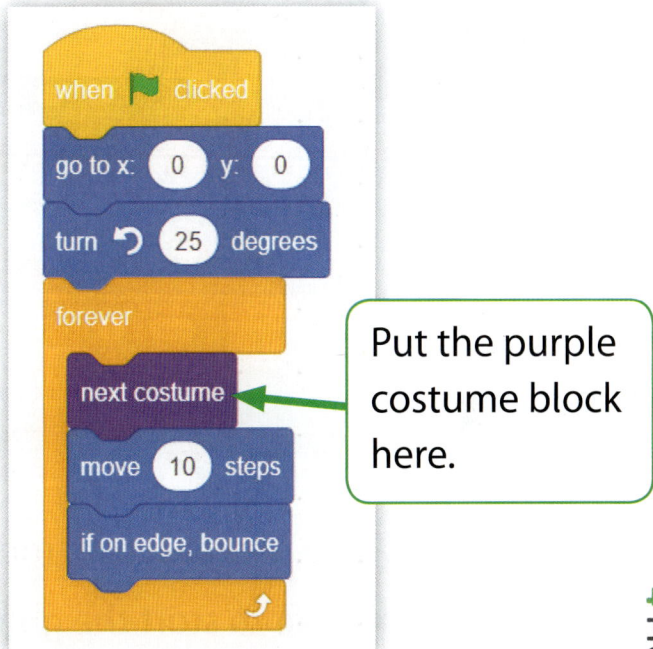

Put the purple costume block here.

Make the program start. What is different?

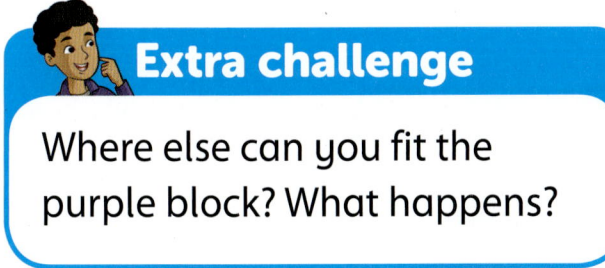

Extra challenge

Where else can you fit the purple block? What happens?

4.4 Extra sprites

In this lesson

You will learn:
→ to add an extra sprite to a program.

You have seen this program before. It is called the Hedgehog Game. Scratch must dodge the hedgehog.

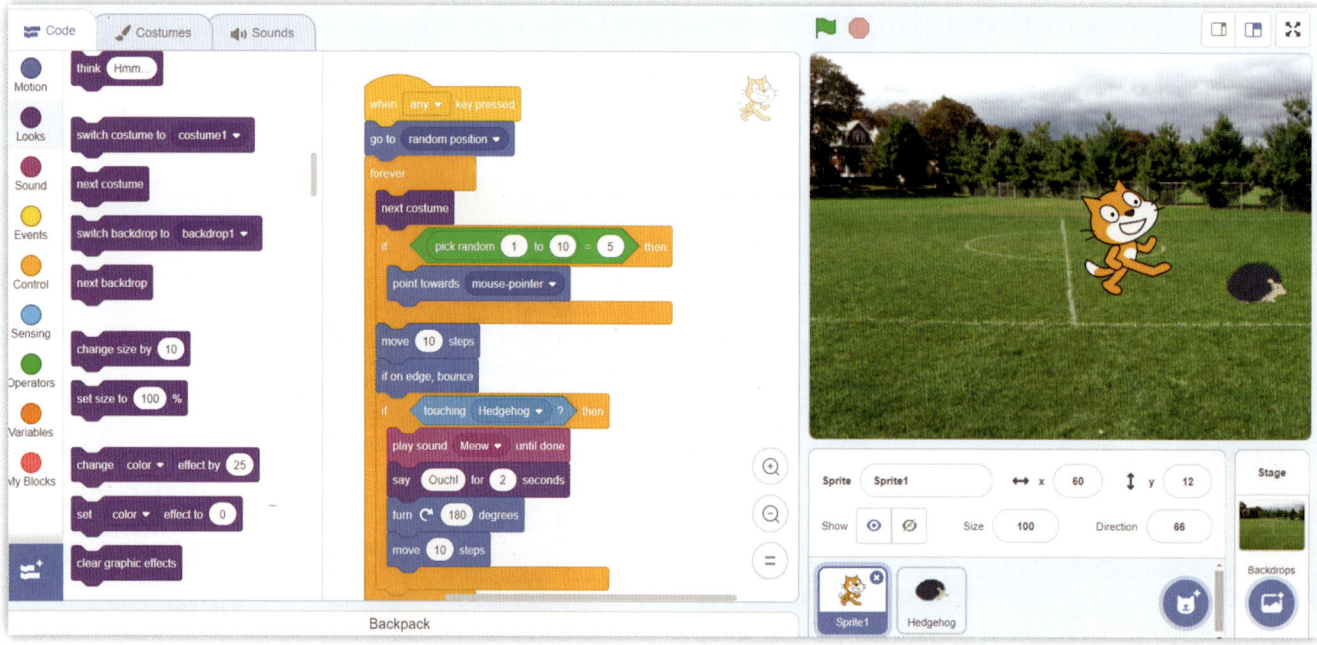

Scratch is a sprite. The program makes the sprite move.

Press the space bar to start the game.

There are two sprites in this game. Now you will add an extra hedgehog to the game.

Be creative

Draw a picture of Scratch and the hedgehogs.

 **Activity**

You will add another hedgehog to the game.

This part of the screen shows the sprites.

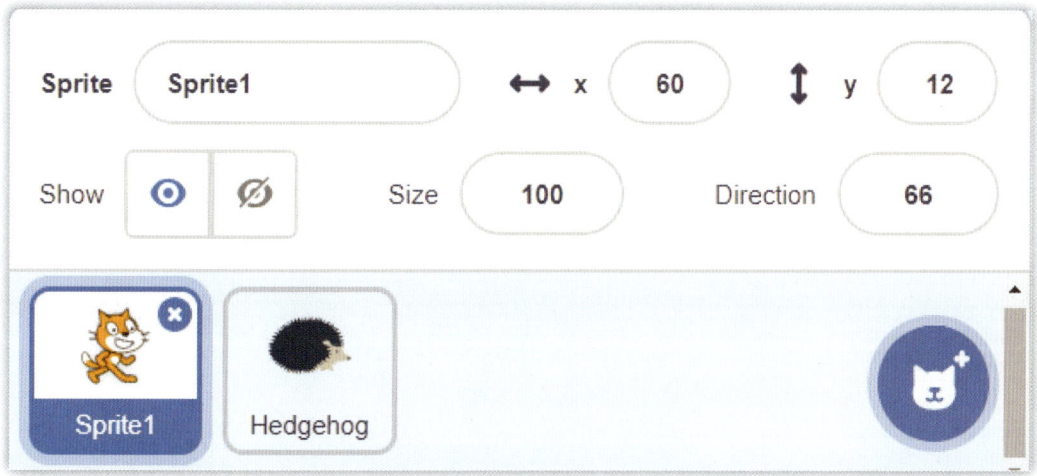

Move the pointer to the hedgehog.

Right-click the mouse. Right-click means to click the right button on the mouse.

You will see this menu.

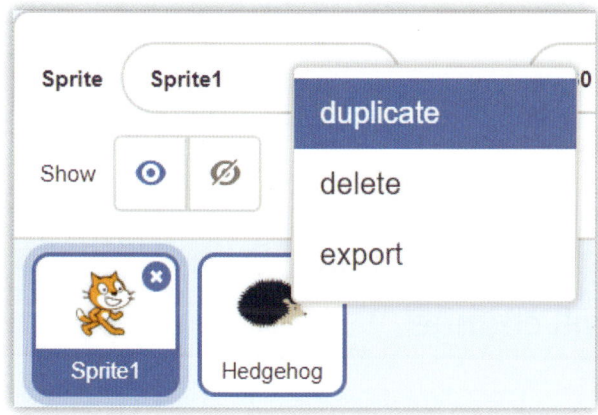

Choose **duplicate**. Duplicate means to make two.

Click anywhere on the screen, then press the space bar to start the game. Now there are two hedgehogs.

 **Extra challenge**

Can you add more hedgehogs to the game? Don't make it too hard for Scratch!

 **Think again** A classmate wants to make a copy of a sprite. Tell her how to do it.

4.5 Find a new block

In this lesson

You will learn:

→ how to find the block you want.

The program looks like this. The program will start when you press any key.

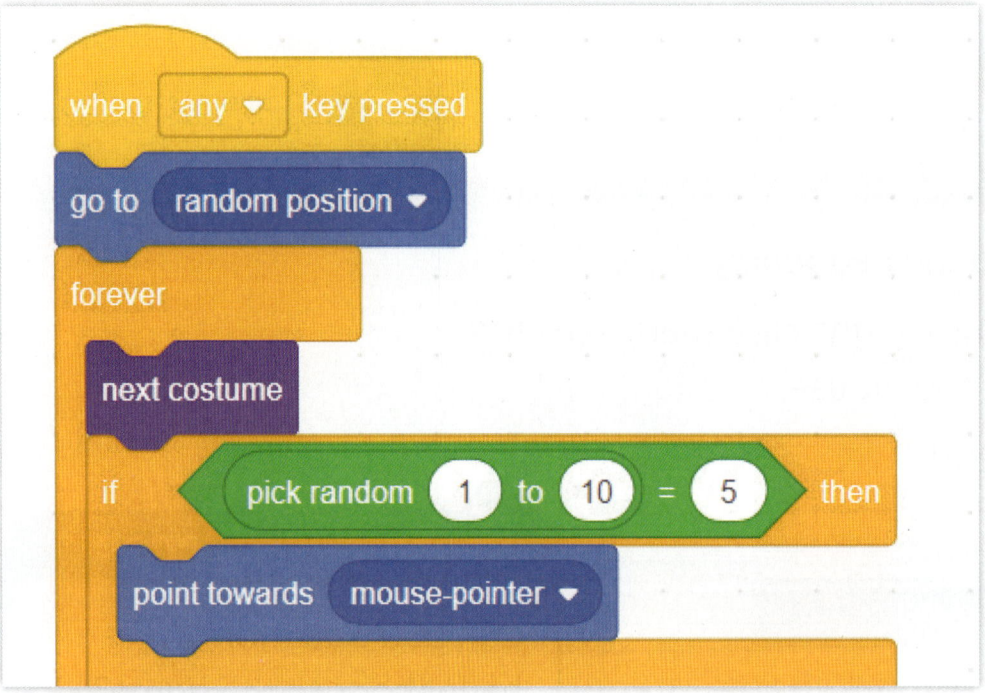

The first block is a start block.

Now you will change the start block. You will change the start block to the green flag block.

New blocks are stored on the left of the screen.

Extra challenge

Click on the hedgehog sprite. Change the start block for the hedgehog.

Think again Say the different ways you can start the game.

 **Activity**

On the left are coloured dots. Click on the yellow dot.

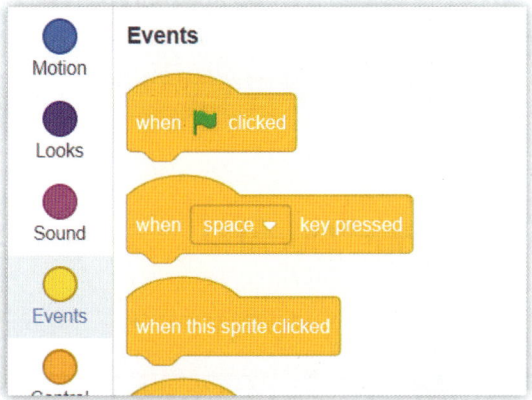

There are lots of start blocks. Find the green flag block.

Drag the block to the program. Drag means to hold down the mouse button and move the mouse.

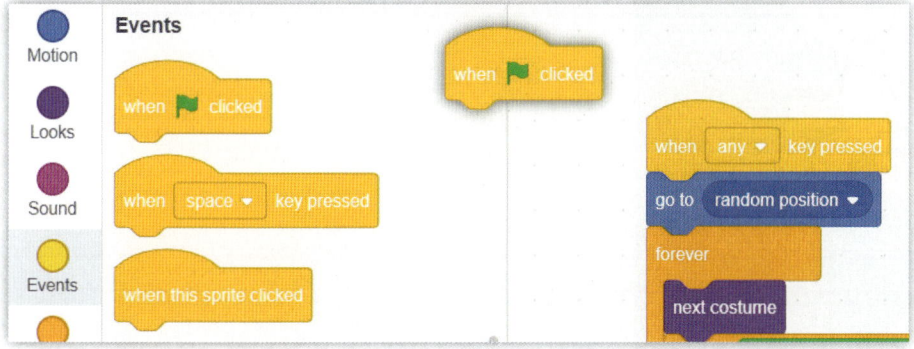

Pull the program blocks away from the old start block. Fit the program to the green flag block.

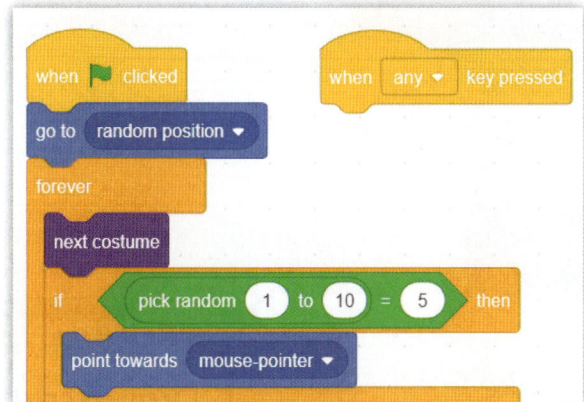

Play the game. The green flag will start the game.

4.6 What Scratch says

In this lesson

You will learn:

→ how to change what Scratch says.

When Scratch touches a hedgehog, he says "Ouch!".

The block that makes Scratch talk looks like this.

Now you will change the block. Make Scratch say something else.

Be creative

Draw Scratch saying the word you chose.

 **Activity**

Find the block where Scratch says: "Ouch!".

Find the word.

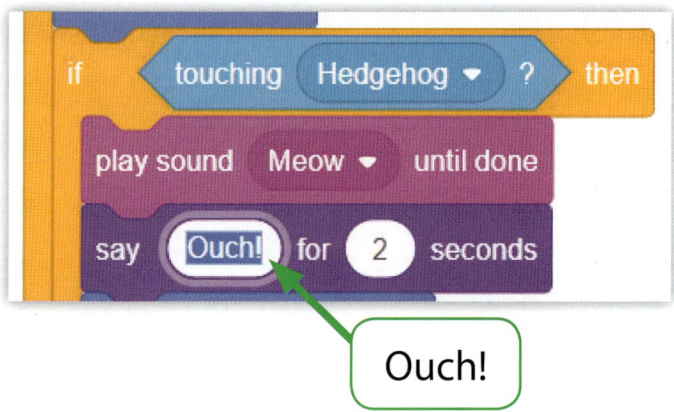

Click on the word. Type a new word.

Play the game. Scratch will say the new word instead of "Ouch!".

 **Explore more**

Talk to people about computer games. Do they like to play computer games? Find out why.

 **Extra challenge**

Some blocks have numbers in them. Change some numbers. See how changing some numbers changes the game.

Check what you know

You have learned
→ about blocks that make a program
→ to make changes to a program.

Here is a Scratch program.

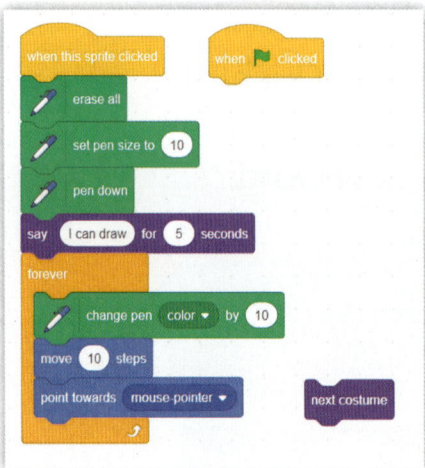

Do as many of these activities as you can.

1 Start the program and move the mouse to see what happens.

2 Change the start block of this program.

3 Add the extra purple block to the program.

4 Change the program so the sprite says "Hello".

Write or tell the teacher what you did.

Test

Here is a Scratch program.

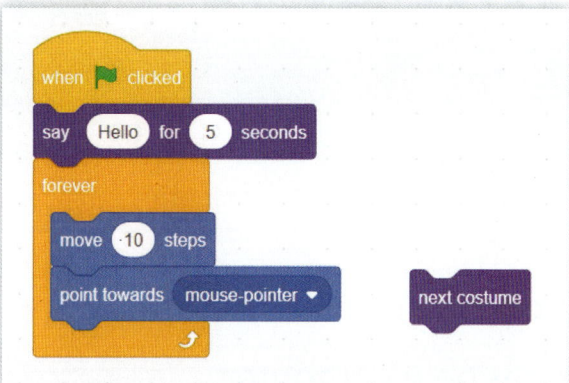

🔴 Point to the block that makes the program start.

🟢 What do you do to make this program start?

🔵 Say one change you could make to the program.

Self-evaluation

- 🔴 I answered test question 1.
- 🔴 I did activity 1.
- 🔴 The teacher saw me work quietly and safely.
- 🟢 I answered test questions 1 and 2.
- 🟢 I did more than one activity.
- 🟢 I told the teacher about what I did.
- 🔵 I answered all the test questions.
- 🔵 I did all the activities.
- 🔵 I explained what I did.

Re-read any parts of the unit you feel unsure about. Try the test and activities again – can you do more this time?

5 Multimedia: Funny faces

You will learn
- how to draw lines and shapes on a computer
- how to colour images on a computer
- how to move images around the screen.

What do you like to draw? You can use a computer to draw and paint.

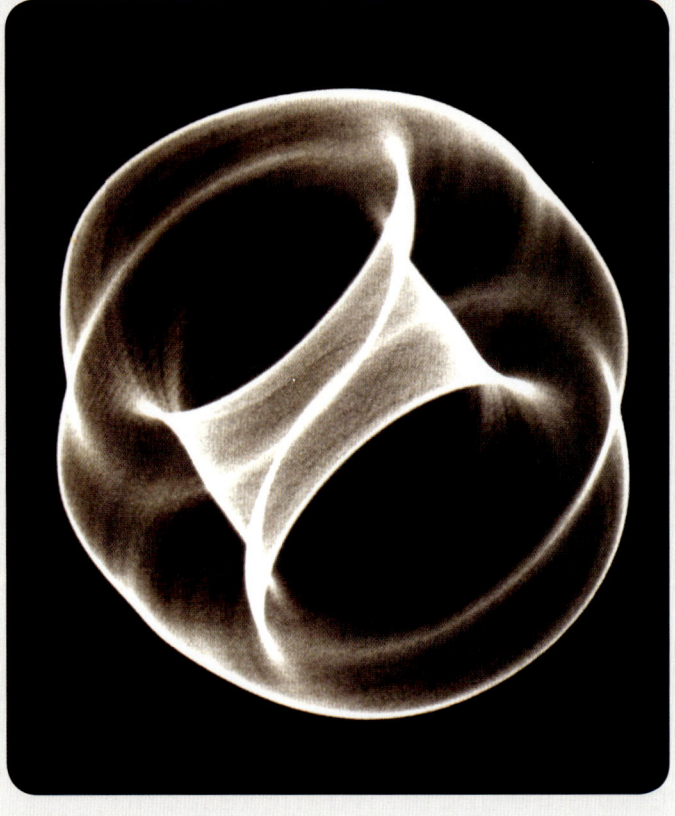

Talk about...
People use computers to change the way they look in a photograph. What do you think about this?

Learning outcomes: Make simple images using computer software

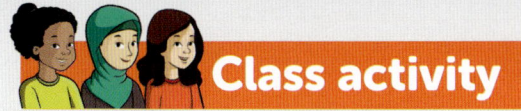

Class activity

Look at a magazine, book or newspaper.

Which pictures were drawn using a computer?

Which pictures were drawn by hand?

> canvas   toolbar
> shape   image   file
> double-click

Did you know?

People have been using computers to draw and colour since the 1950s. Ben Laposky used a machine for measuring electronic signals to draw a beautiful **shape**. A shape is the outline of something, for example, a circle or a square.

5.1 The canvas

In this lesson

You will learn:

→ how to make a drawing on a computer.

Drawing with the computer

You can use your mouse to draw on a computer. If you have a tablet you can draw with your finger.

You can draw lines and shapes.

Draw lines

Here is a drawing program. The white area is called the **canvas**. The canvas is where you can draw.

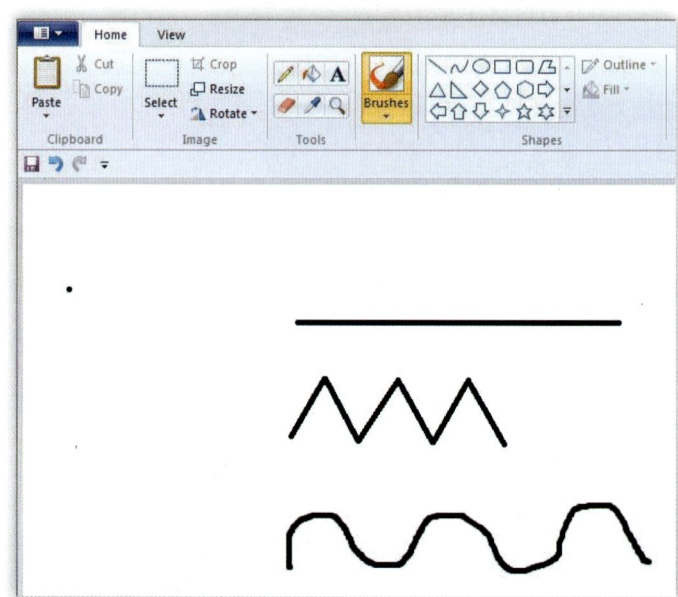

Above the canvas is a toolbar. The **toolbar** is a line of buttons. Click on a button to choose what the computer will do.

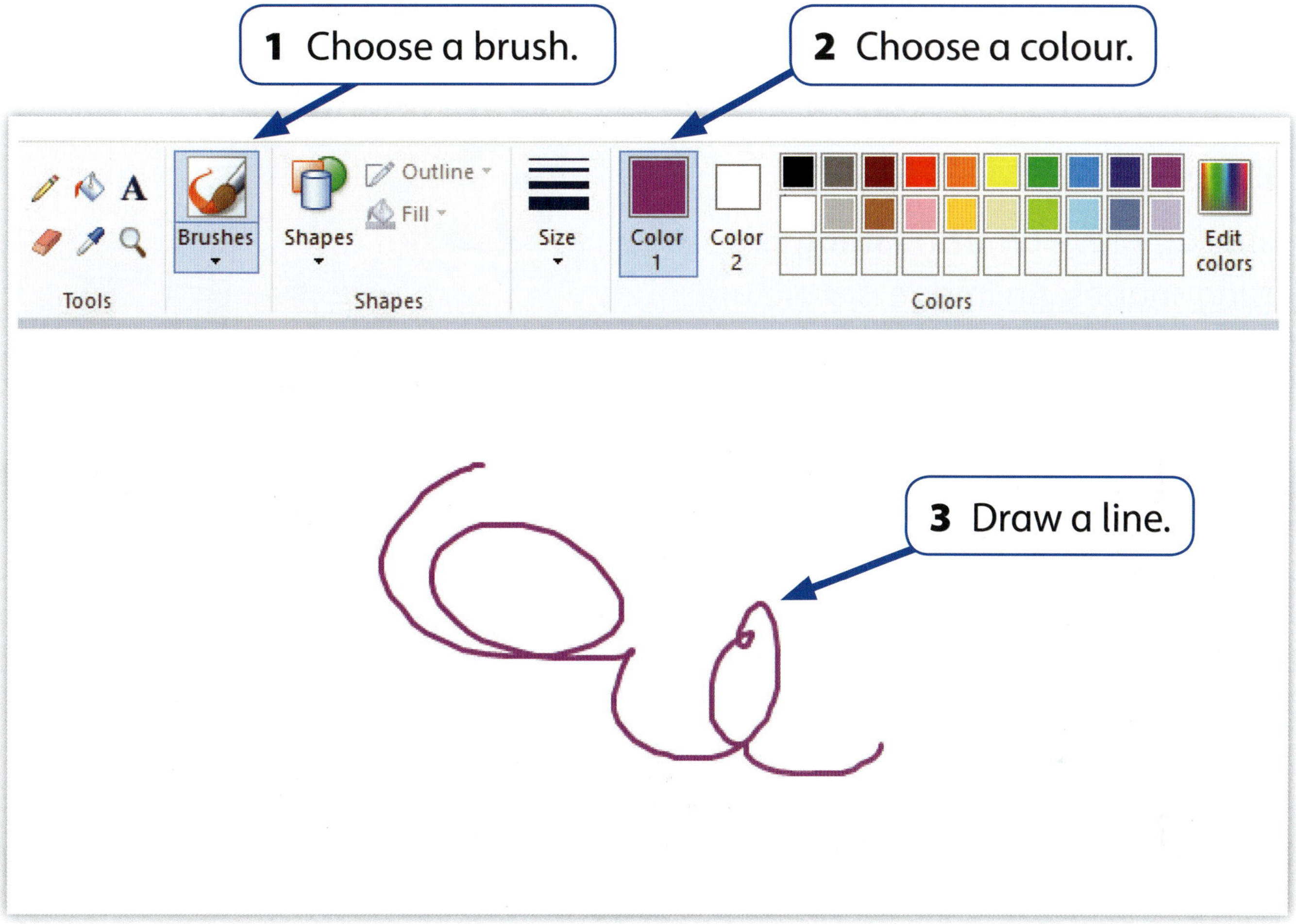

1 Choose a brush.

2 Choose a colour.

3 Draw a line.

 **Activity**

Draw a face on the canvas.

 **Extra challenge**

Which button changes the size of the brush? See what happens when you click the button.

 **Think again**

Plan a drawing on paper, then try to make the drawing on the screen.

5 Multimedia: Funny faces

5.2 Drawing shapes

In this lesson

You will learn:
→ how to draw shapes.

Shapes

You can make amazing **images** using shapes. An image is a picture or part of a picture.

This image uses squares and rectangles.

Draw a shape

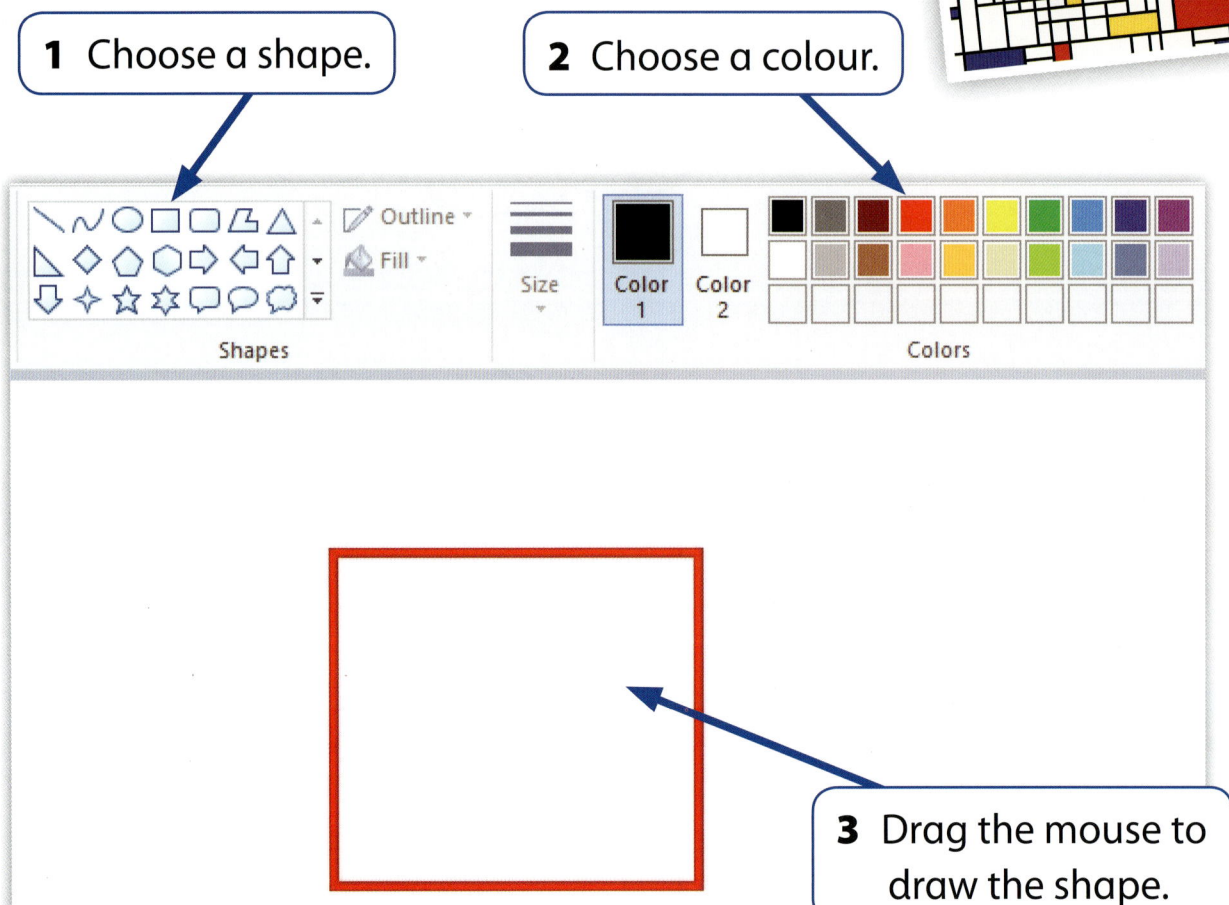

1 Choose a shape.

2 Choose a colour.

3 Drag the mouse to draw the shape.

Fill with colour

The paint pot shape 'pours' paint into the shapes you make.

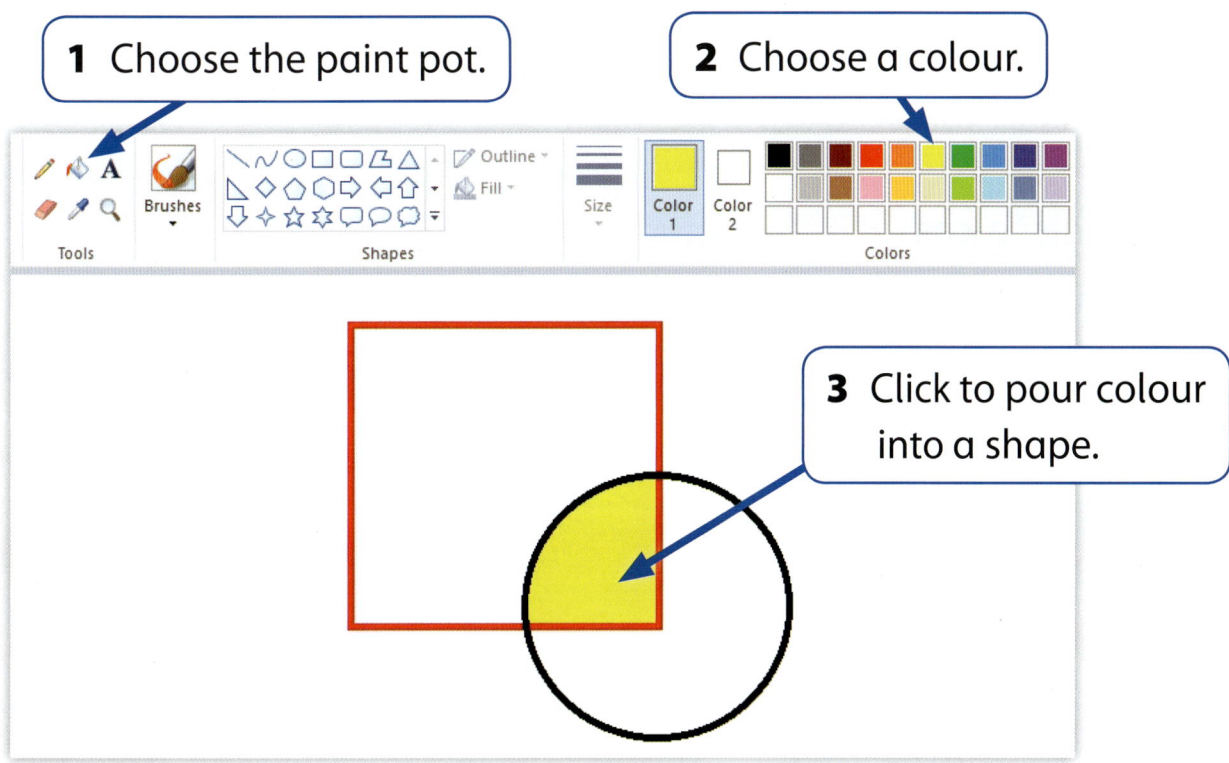

1 Choose the paint pot.

2 Choose a colour.

3 Click to pour colour into a shape.

Activity

Draw a shape on your screen. Fill the shape with colour.

Extra challenge

Draw shapes that overlap. Use colours to fill the areas where they overlap.

Think again What feeling does your image give you? Do you think different colours make you feel different feelings?

5.3 Erasing and undoing

In this lesson

You will learn:

→ how to rub out mistakes.

Making mistakes

Drawing can be hard. We sometimes make mistakes. What do you do if you make a mistake when you draw?

Erase

You can use an eraser to rub out a mistake on paper.

A drawing program has an eraser too.

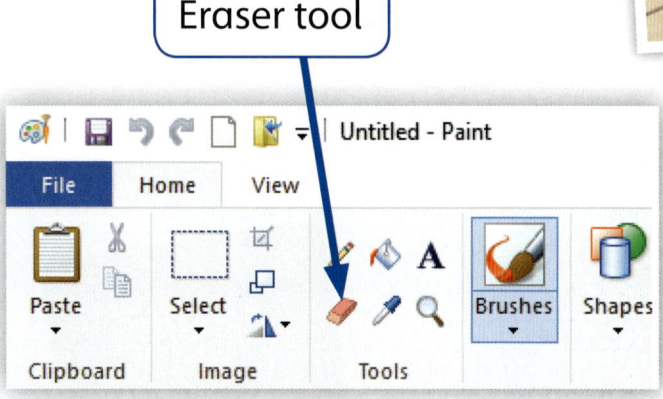

Eraser tool

Undo

What if you do something wrong in an image? 'Undo' reverses what you did.

Press and hold down the 'Control' key on your keyboard.

Now press the letter 'Z' on your keyboard.

 **Activity**

Draw a face with a circle for a nose. Erase it and put a triangle instead. Which is best?

 Extra challenge

Draw a face by putting shapes together. Now draw one with a line. Which is best?

Think again

Artists use many different shapes for noses.

Can you see all the shapes and colours this artist has used?

5.4 Save for another time

In this lesson

You will learn:

→ how to save your work.

What does save mean?

When you switch the computer off your work is lost. But you can save your work for another time.

Draw an image on the screen. Then save the image.

How to save

Find the 'Save' button. The 'Save' button is at the top of the screen.

Click on the 'Save' button. The button will save your work.

File name

Your work is saved as a **file**. A file is a place to keep information on a computer. Type a name for the file.

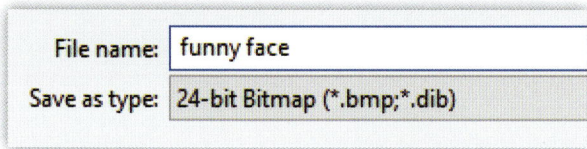

The file name should remind you what is in the file.

New image

Now your work is saved you can start a new image. Click the 'New' button to make a new image.

You will see a new blank canvas ready to make your next image.

Draw a face. Save the face using the file name: 'face'.

Extra challenge

Start a new image. Save the new image using a new file name.

Think again What makes a good file name?

5.5 Bring back your file

In this lesson

You will learn:

→ how to open a saved file

→ how to make changes and save again.

Open a file

When you start work you see a new empty screen. Now you will open the file you saved last time. Click the 'Open' button.

You will see all the images you have saved.

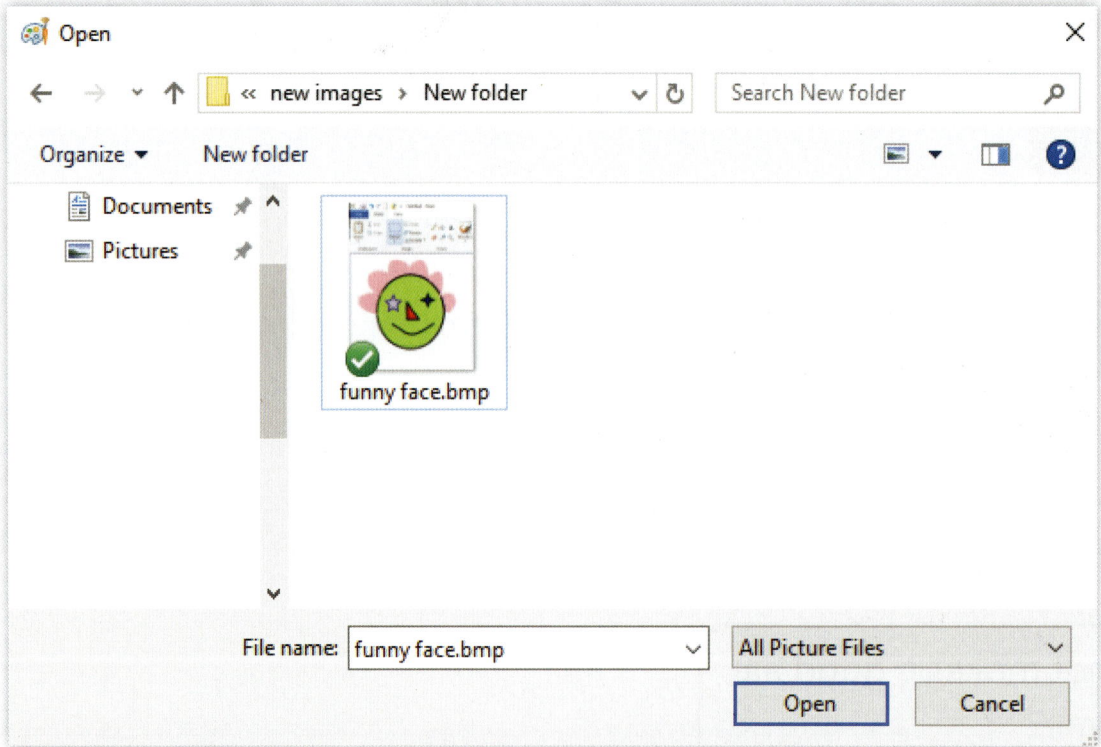

Double-click the file you want to open. Double-click means click twice quickly.

Make changes

Now you can make changes to the image. You can use the eraser to rub things out. Or you can draw on top of the old image.

Save with a new name

Click on the word 'File' at the top of the screen. Choose 'Save as' from the menu.

Type a new file name.

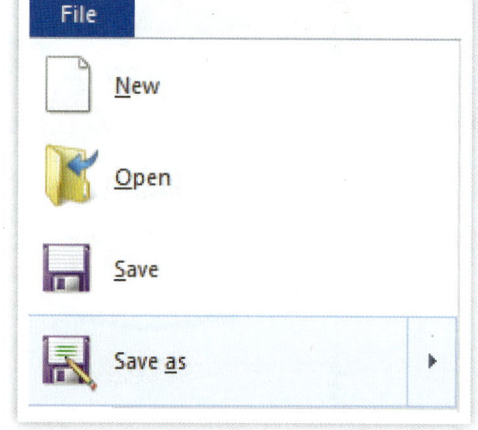

Open the file you made last time. Make one change and save the file using the 'Save' button.

Extra challenge

Use 'Save as' to save your file using a new file name.

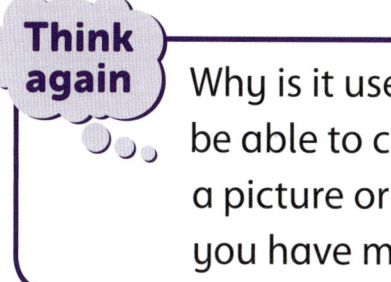

Think again Why is it useful to be able to change a picture or slide you have made?

5.6 Move and swap

In this lesson

You will learn:

→ how to select and move parts of the image.

Swap noses

A student drew two funny faces. Then she decided to swap noses.

Select

You can select part of the image that you made. Click on the 'Select' button.

Now drag the mouse. You can drag a line around any part of the screen.

Move

Now you can drag the selected part. You can move it to a new place. Or a new face!

The student swapped noses between the two faces.

 **Activity**

Draw two funny faces and swap noses like you see here.

 **Extra challenge**

Draw two animals, such as a cat and a mouse. Use select and move to swap the animals' tails.

 **Explore more**

Paint a funny face using lots of colours and shapes. Now try to make the face using computer software. Make a display in class of both types of image.

Check what you know

You have learned
- how to draw lines and shapes on a computer
- how to colour images on a computer
- how to move images around the screen.

Test

Here is an image made by a student using a computer.

Show or tell to answer the questions.

1. Show or tell how to make a star shape.
2. Show or tell how you could rub out the blue star.
3. Show or tell how you could move the red star to a new place.

 **Activities**

This image shows a house. It is made of a triangle and a square.

1 Draw the square shape of the house. Draw a triangle roof.

2 Add windows and a door.

3 Make the image more colourful. If you have time, add something else to your house. You could add a chimney, curtains or a door handle.

Self-evaluation

- I answered test question 1.
- I did activity 1.
- I answered test questions 1 and 2.
- I did activities 1 and 2.
- I answered all the test questions.
- I did all the activities.

Re-read any parts of the unit you feel unsure about. Try the test and activities again – can you do more this time?

6 Numbers and data: Toys long ago

You will learn
→ how to put words and numbers into the computer
→ how to change words and numbers stored on the computer.

Computers can store numbers. Computers can work out the answers to sums.

Talk about…
What kinds of toys do you think children had long ago?

Learning outcomes: Enter words and numbers into the computer

Class activity

Your teacher will say the names of different toys children played with long ago. Put your hand up if you like the toy.

Which toy gets the most hands up?

cell   spreadsheet
label   value   data
edit   select

Did you know?

The numbers we use in spreadsheets today, 1, 2, 3 and so on, were developed in India and Arabia over one thousand years ago.

6.1 Toys from the past

In this lesson

You will learn:
- how to find numbers using counting
- how to record your answers.

Counting

Imagine you are an archaeologist.

An archaeologist is a person who finds out about the past by digging up things people have made. They go on digs to find old things.

Imagine you are on a dig and you find some old toys.

 **Activity**

Look at all these old toys you have found!

Write the word 'ball'. Next to it, write down how many balls you see.

Write the word 'bear'. Next to it, write down how many bears you see.

Write the word 'car'. Next to it, write down how many cars you see.

 **Explore more**

Count the toys you see in your home, or in a newspaper or magazine.

What different kinds of toys can you see?

Digital citizen of the future

What sorts of jobs use numbers?

6.2 Cells

In this lesson

You will learn:

- what a spreadsheet is
- how to choose a cell in a spreadsheet.

A spreadsheet

A **spreadsheet** looks like a grid on the screen. There are lines and boxes.

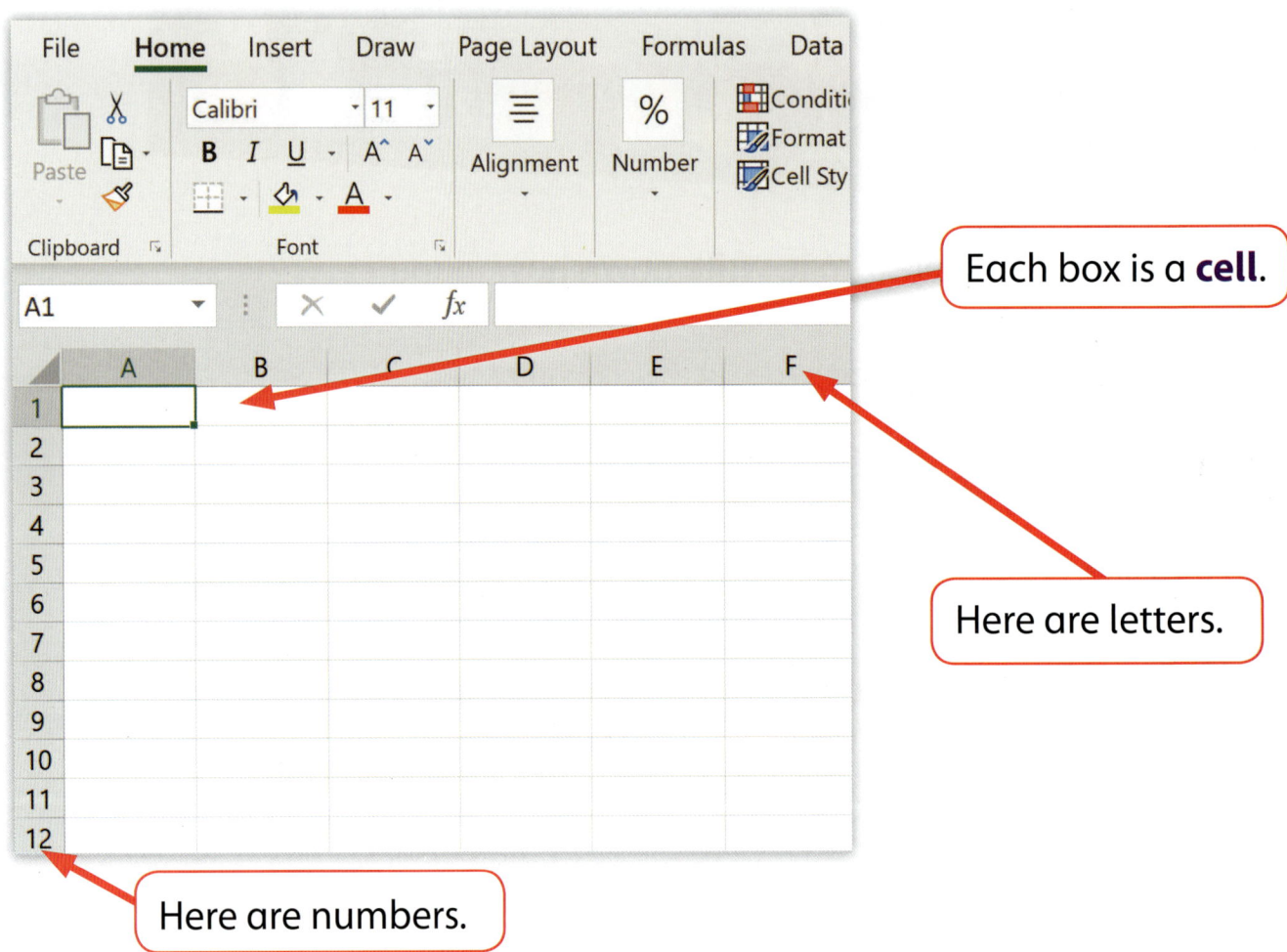

Each box is a **cell**.

Here are letters.

Here are numbers.

You can name each cell using letters and numbers. The first cell is A1. The cell is in the A column. The cell is in row 1.

Select a cell

Move the mouse pointer to a cell. The mouse pointer looks like a cross.

Click the left mouse button. You **select** the cell. Select means you have chosen the cell.

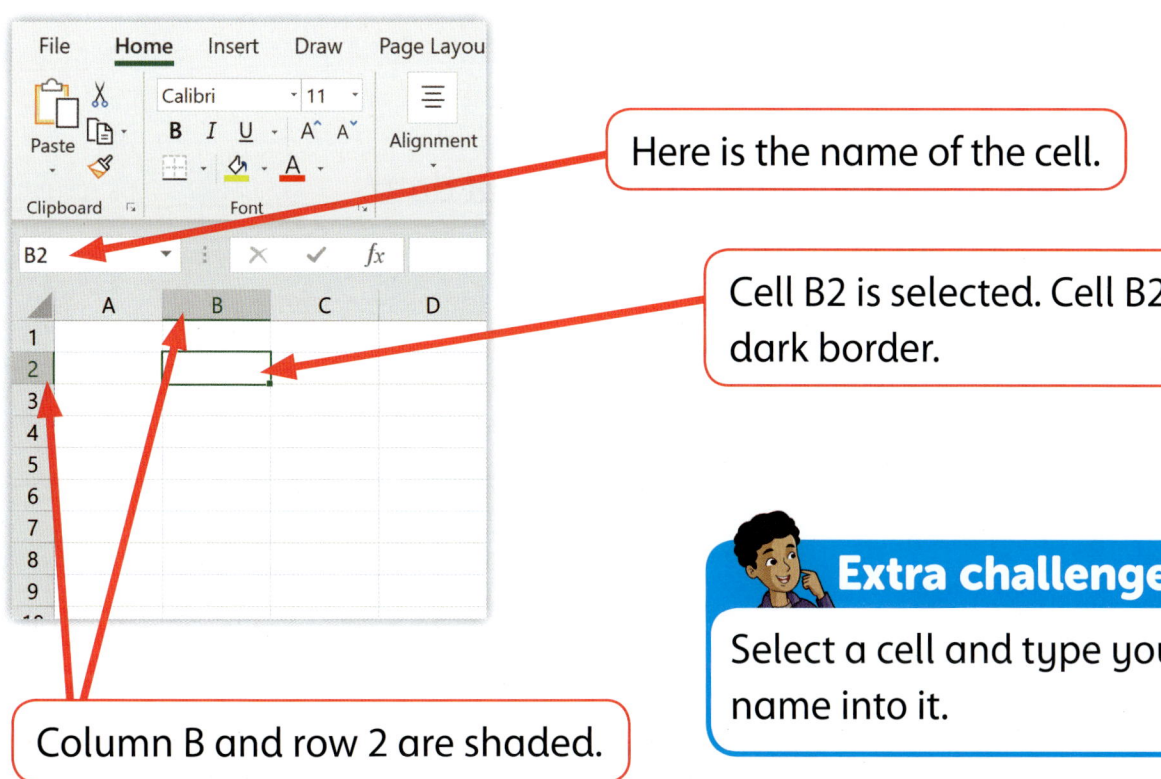

Here is the name of the cell.

Cell B2 is selected. Cell B2 has a dark border.

Column B and row 2 are shaded.

Extra challenge

Select a cell and type your name into it.

 **Activity**

You will see a spreadsheet open on your screen.

Move the mouse pointer to these cells.

A1   C3   E8   B4   F10

Click to select each cell.

Think again

Data is the name for information that we type into a computer. Names are one example of data. Can you think of any other types of data?

6.3 Labels

In this lesson

You will learn:

→ what labels are

→ how to enter labels into a spreadsheet.

Labels

You can use **labels** in a spreadsheet to talk about data. A label is a word, or a small number of words.

The top of a spreadsheet looks like this.

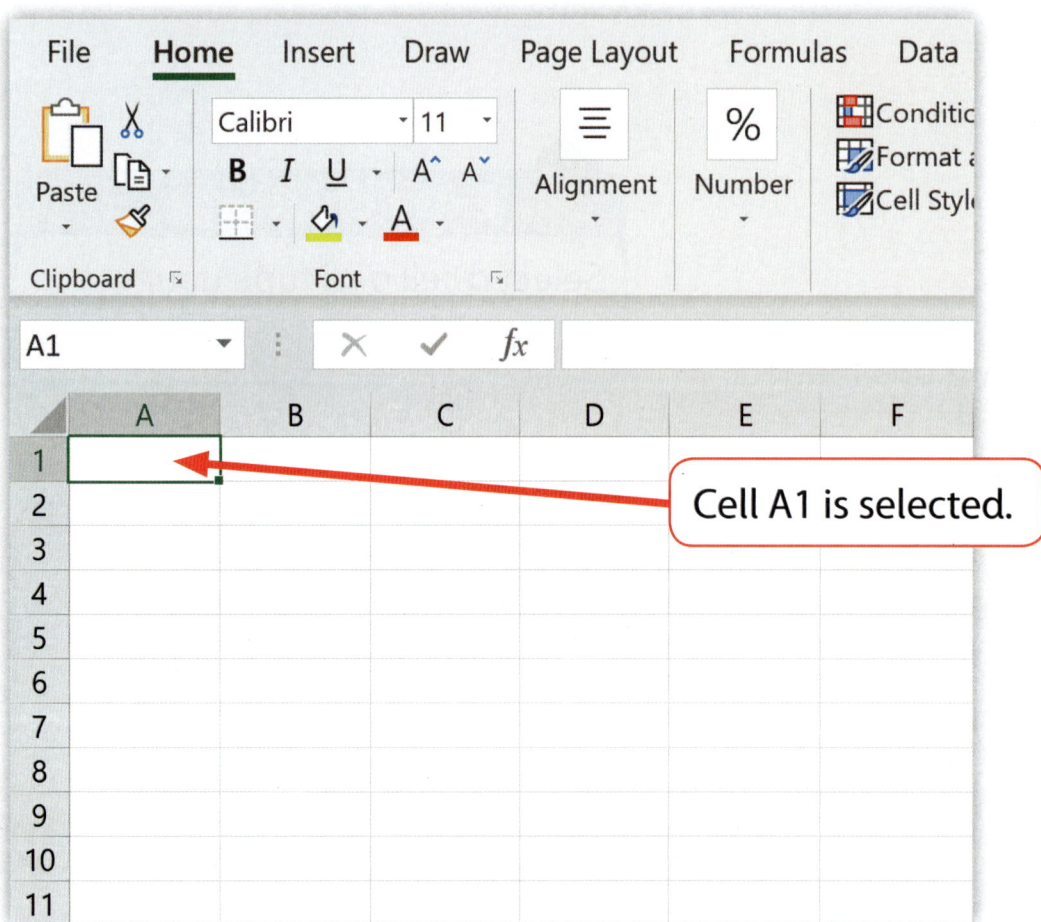

Cell A1 is selected.

 **Activity**

Imagine you are an archaeologist finding old toys. You want to make a list of the toys you have found. You can enter labels by typing them in a cell.

Click cell A1.

Type the label: 'Toys'.

Press 'Enter'.

Your spreadsheet should look like this.

Think again Which cell in this spreadsheet has a label in it?

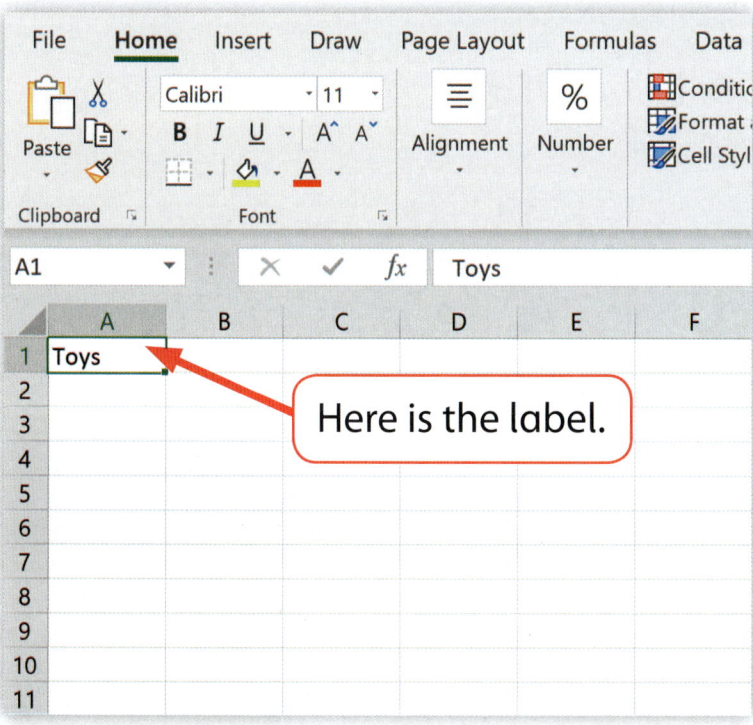

Here is the label.

Save your spreadsheet as a file called: 'Toys'.

This is an example of an ancient toy. It is a dove on wheels from the 5th century BCE.

6.4 Making a list

In this lesson

You will learn:

→ how to make a list in a spreadsheet.

Open a file

Open your file called 'Toys'.

Click 'File' with the left-hand mouse button.

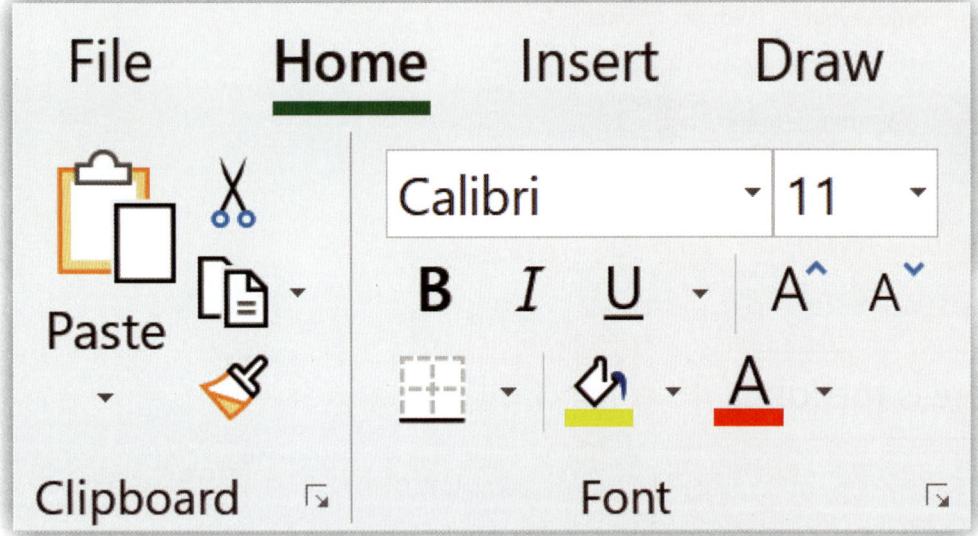

Click 'Open' with the left-hand mouse button.

Click the file called 'Toys' with the left-hand mouse button. You might need to double-click. **Double-click** means click two times quickly.

Imagine you are an archaeologist. You will add the labels for toys you have found on your dig.

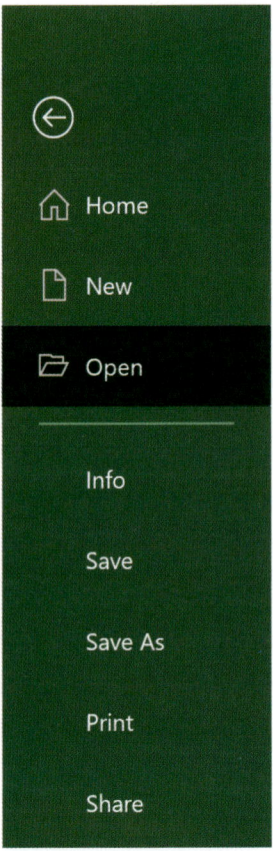

 **Activity**

Make a list in your spreadsheet of the types of toys that children played with long ago.

In cell A2 type: 'ball'.	
In cell A3 type: 'doll'.	
In cell A4 type: 'game'.	
In cell A5 type: 'animal'.	

 **Think again** Say one more type of toy you could add to this list.

6.5 Number values

In this lesson

You will learn:
- what spreadsheet values are
- how to enter values into a spreadsheet.

Numbers in a spreadsheet are called **values**.

Each cell holds a label or a value.

Now you are going to type in the values for each toy.

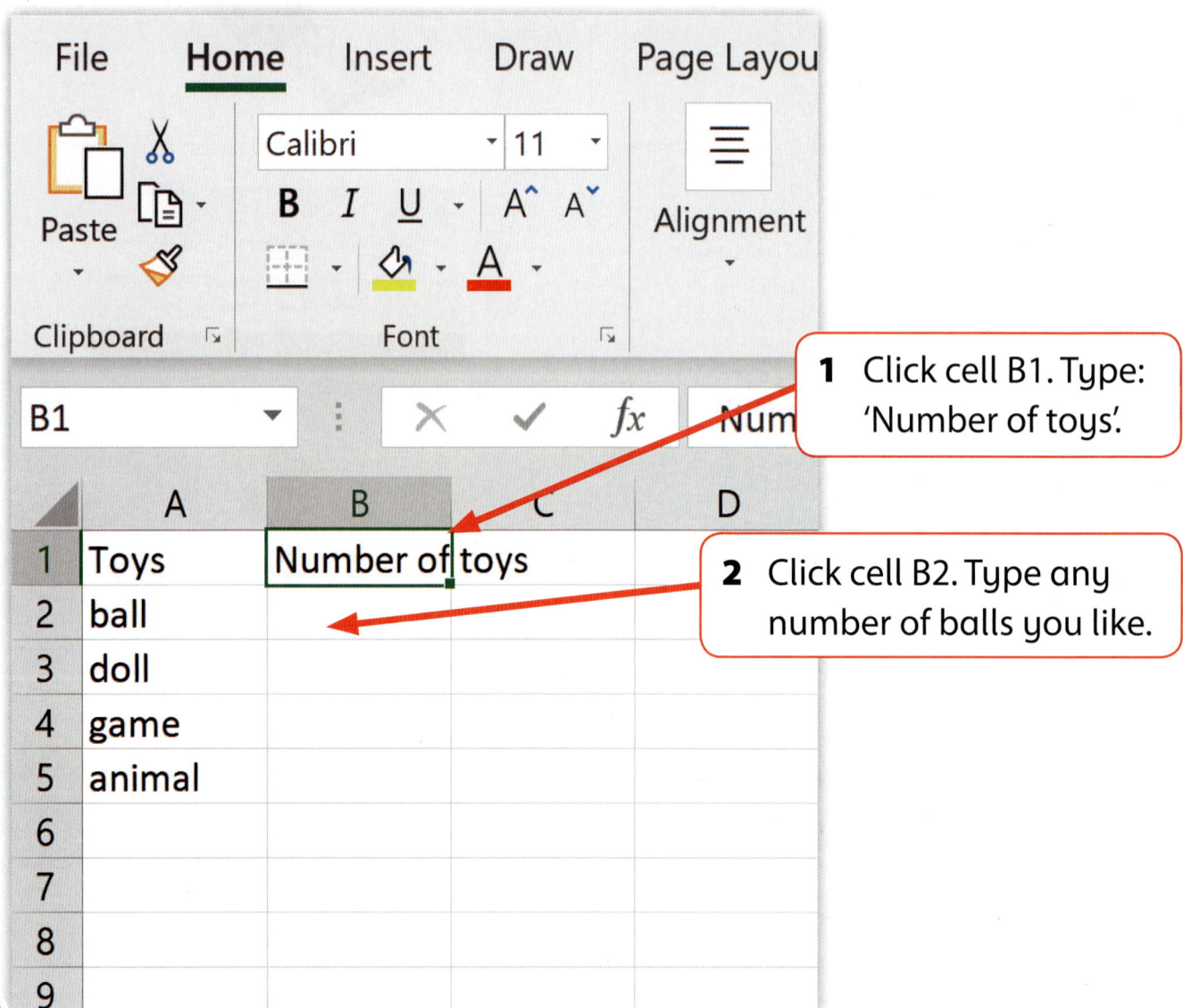

1. Click cell B1. Type: 'Number of toys'.
2. Click cell B2. Type any number of balls you like.

 **Activity**

Type number values next to each label in your spreadsheet. You can choose any numbers you like. Think about how many toys children might have had long ago.

Remember to save your file.

Digital citizen of the future

This is the type of ball children played with in Ancient Egypt.

Do you think children long ago had many toys? Or did they just have a few?

What kinds of toys can you imagine in the future?

 **Think again** Think of two more toys you could add to column A in the spreadsheet.

6.6 Editing

In this lesson

You will learn:

→ how to edit values in a spreadsheet.

Changing values

Imagine you are an archaeologist. You have put information about old toys into a spreadsheet.

Now imagine you have found more toys!

You need to change the values in the spreadsheet. When you **edit**, you make changes to a file.

Open your file called 'Toys'.

Look at the labels and values in the spreadsheet.

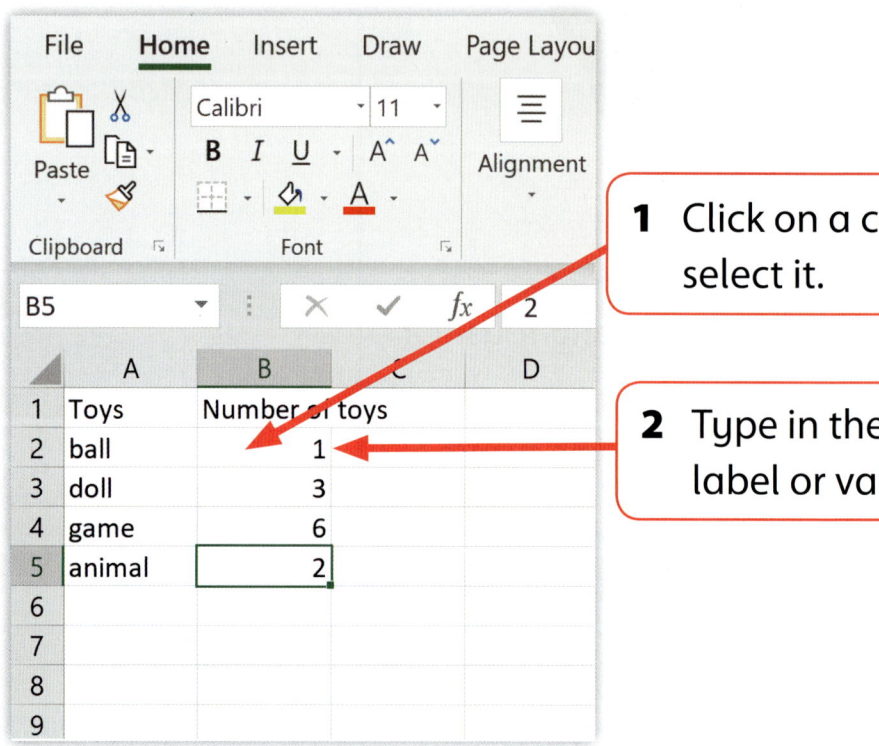

1. Click on a cell to select it.

2. Type in the new label or value.

Now press 'Enter' on the keyboard.

 **Activity**

Change the values in your spreadsheet.

Add one ball.	
Add three dolls.	
Add two games.	
Add one marble.	
Add one animal.	

Save your file as: 'Found toys edited'.

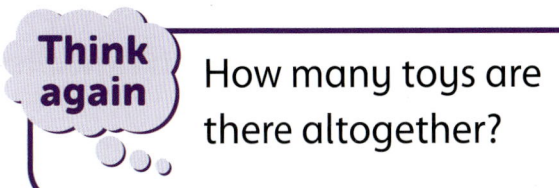

Think again How many toys are there altogether?

Check what you know

You have learned

→ how to put words and numbers into the computer

→ how to change words and numbers stored on the computer.

This spreadsheet is called 'Toys Test'. Make sure it is open and ready to use.

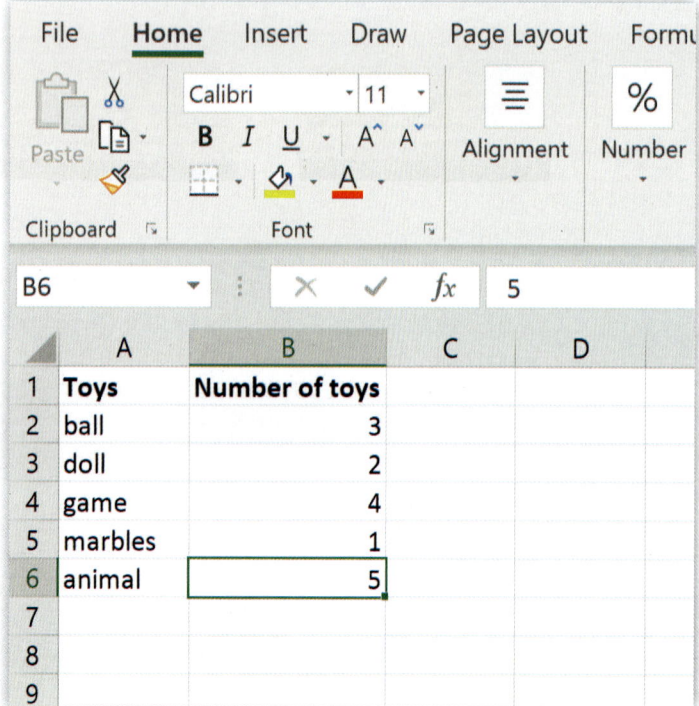

1. Type the word 'Teddy' in cell A7.
2. Type the number '1' in cell B7.
3. Type your name in an empty cell.
4. Save the file with a new file name.

Test

Show or tell how you work with a spreadsheet.

- **1** Draw the thing you use to select a cell.
- **2** Name the thing you use to type words.
- **3** A cell is called C3. Explain what that means.

Self-evaluation

- I answered test question 1.
- I did the first activity.
- I answered test questions 1 and 2.
- I did activities 1 and 2.
- I answered all the test questions.
- I did all the activities.

Re-read any parts of the unit you feel unsure about. Try the test and activities again – can you do more this time?

Glossary

backdrop the backdrop is the picture at the back of the stage when you make a program with Scratch

block a Scratch program is made of blocks. The blocks are shapes that fit together. Each block makes the computer do one thing

browser software that helps us find and see information on the internet

canvas the area of the screen where you draw and paint when you make a picture using software

cell each box in a spreadsheet

computer a machine that can work quickly to make changes to data

content anything we see or create, for example, on the internet

costume in the Scratch program the sprite can have different looks. For example, Scratch can have his legs in two different positions. Each different look is called a costume

courteous to be polite and think about other people

data pieces of information, for example, numbers stored in a spreadsheet

double-click to click twice quickly

drag to hold down the mouse button and move the mouse. When you drag, you move something across the screen

drag and drop to move something across the screen and place it somewhere else

duplicate to make two of something

edit to make changes to a file

file a place to keep information on a computer

hyperlink if you click on a hyperlink, you move to a different place in a website or on the internet

icon a little picture. When you click on an icon the computer does something

image a picture or part of a picture

input something you do to control the computer or put data into the computer. You can use the keyboard and mouse for input

internet computers all over the world are connected. We call all these connected computers the internet

keyboard buttons with letters, numbers and symbols that you use with your computer. When you press on the keyboard buttons, the letters, numbers and symbols show on the screen

label words in a spreadsheet

laptop a small computer you can carry

menu a list of things that you can choose from, for example, on a website

mouse a small tool you move with your hand or finger to move the mouse pointer on the screen. A mouse is used for input

mouse pointer a little arrow. When you move the mouse, the mouse pointer moves too

output something that comes out of the computer. The computer makes output, for example, sounds or pictures on the screen

personal information information about your life, for example, your name, your address or your school. Personal information can be words as well as pictures

program a set of instructions. The instructions tell the computer what to do

right-click click the right button of a mouse

run when you run a program the computer carries out the commands in the program

Scratch a programming language for children. The programs are made of blocks. Each block stands for a command

screen the place on your computer where you can see the things you type, or other information

scrolling documents and web pages can be quite big. You can't see the whole page on the screen. Scrolling lets you look through the page a bit at a time

search engine software that searches for websites using words that you type into the computer

select you choose an item on the screen by clicking it with the mouse. Then you can work with that item. One example is a spreadsheet cell

shape the outline of something, for example, a circle or a square

sound output the computer makes sounds. These sounds are sound output

spreadsheet a grid of cells with rows and columns that you put words and numbers into

sprite a sprite is a picture on screen. A program makes the sprite move. Scratch the cat is a sprite

stage the stage is where a sprite moves

start block a type of Scratch block that shows what action will start the program

technology any machine that people use to do tasks or solve a problem

title bar the place that shows the name of the file you are working with, for example, the name of a web page

toolbar a collection of icons. If you click on an icon the computer will do something

value an item of data; a spreadsheet can hold number values

visual output the screen shows visual output

web page a page on the internet

website a set of web pages